Unbound by Time

T0159320

Cowley Publications is a ministry of the Society of Saint John the Evangelist, a religious community of men in the Episcopal Church. Emerging from the Society's tradition of prayer, theological reflection, and diversity of mission, the press is centered in the rich heritage of the Anglican Communion.

Cowley Publications seeks to provide books, audio cassettes, CDs, and other resources for the ongoing theological exploration and spiritual development of the Episcopal Church and others in the body of Christ. To this end, it is dedicated to developing a new generation of theological writers, encouraging them to produce timely, creative, and stimulating publications of excellence, and making these publications available widely, reaching both clergy and lay persons.

Unbound by Time
Isaiah Still Speaks

WILLIAM L. HOLLADAY

A COWLEY PUBLICATIONS BOOK
ROWMAN & LITTLEFIELD PUBLISHERS, INC.
Lanham • Chicago • New York • Toronto • Plymouth, UK

Library of Congress Cataloging-in-Publication Data:
Holladay, William Lee.
    Unbound by time : Isaiah still speaks / William L. Holladay.
        p. cm.
Includes bibliographical references.
    ISBN 1-56101-204-1 (pbk. : alk. paper)
    1. Bible. O.T. Isaiah—Criticism, interpretation, etc. I. Title.
BS1515.52 .H65 2002
224'.106—dc21

                                                    2002006001

Scripture quotations are taken from *The New Revised Standard
Version* of the Bible, © 1989, by the Division of Christian
Education of the National Council of the Churches of Christ in
the United States of America. Used by Permission.

Cover design: Gary Ragaglia

This book was printed in the United States of America on acid-free
paper.

A Cowley Publications Book
Published by Rowman & Littlefield Publishers, Inc.
A wholly owned subsidary of
The Rowman & Littlefield Publishing Group, Inc.
4501 Forbes Boulevard, Suite 200, Lanham, Maryland 20706
http://www.rowmanlittlefield.com

Estover Road, Plymouth PL6 7PY, United Kingdom

Distributed by National Book Network

FOR PATTY

Contents

Introduction

Over twenty years ago a little book of mine appeared with the title *Isaiah, Scroll of a Prophetic Heritage.*[1] It unpacked the original contexts of a great many of the prophetic texts collected over centuries in that long book of sixty-six chapters. In that work I also dealt with how Christians have understood those particular texts from Isaiah that have taken on a crucial role in Christian proclamation.

In recent years I have explored the latter issue more and more—how Christians have heard and might hear Old Testament texts in upbuilding their faith. The result of that exploration was two books: *The Psalms Through Three Thousand Years: Prayerbook of a Cloud of Witnesses*[2] and *Long Ago God Spoke: How Christians May Hear the Old Testament Today.*[3] In turn this exploration has suggested that a book that centers on the same issues in Isaiah might be useful. Hence the present work, a treatment that I hope will prove useful for folk who hear texts from Isaiah, particularly in the course of lectionary readings, and who are not afraid of a few complications in coming to terms with the meanings of these texts. My premise is simple: though the book of Isaiah is bound to specific times and places, being part of the canon of Holy Scripture, it is equally *unbound by time* or place when it is properly proclaimed by people of faith. Isaiah still speaks!

Basic to this enterprise is the explanation, set forth in Chapter 1, of three ways to hear a prophetic text. I am convinced that ordinary Christians are capable of grasping how texts which functioned in one way in the past can function in fresh ways in the present, and that this understanding will allow the texts maximum communicative power for Christian believers. In this work I treat texts taken from the book of Isaiah according to their prominence:

* Of primary importance are the texts that occur for Sundays and the major festivals in the Revised Common Lectionary,[4] the Episcopal Lectionary[5] the Roman Catholic Lectionary[6] and the variations from the Revised Common Lectionary used by the Evangelical Lutheran Church in America.[7]

* Next in importance are the lessons from Isaiah for "Solemnities and Feasts" in the Roman Catholic Sunday Missal, for "Holy Days," "The Common of Saints," and "Various Occasions" in the Episcopal lectionary, and for "Lesser Festivals" in the Lutheran lectionary.

* In third rank are the texts from Isaiah appointed by Roman Catholics and appearing in *The Vatican II Weekday Missal*[8]—the texts for weekdays, for the Proper of Saints, for Commons, for various Ritual Masses (Christian Initiation [Baptism of Adults] Apart from the Easter Vigil and Confirmation, and for Holy Orders), for Masses for Various Needs and Occasions, and for various Votive Masses.

* And fourth are various passages that are employed as "canticles" in the Liturgy of the Hours (morning and evening prayer) for Roman Catholics.[9] I have not attempted to cover the Isaiah texts included in the Daily Office Lectionary of *The Book of Common Prayer* (Episcopal). For an understanding of all these lectionaries, see the notes which follow on page xiii.

This work revolves around three foci.

* The first focus is the thought and words of the original Isaiah, whose career, as we shall see, is to be dated in the second half of the eighth century BCE,[10] in Jerusalem, during a time of great peril for the kingdom of Judah. A basic component of Isaiah's message is God's judgment on the people for their neglect of social justice.

* The second focus is the thought and words of an anonymous prophet conventionally called "Second Isaiah," whose career is to be dated in the second half of the *sixth* century BCE, evidently in Babylon, where he and his fellow exiles were held. In setting forth the work of this Second Isaiah I have accepted the proposal of the British scholar H. G. M. Williamson, that the material from the original Isaiah was edited and to some degree rearranged by the latter in the service of his own message.[11] The center of gravity of that message was not judgment on the people but rather hope for their future.

* And the third focus is the selection of lectionary readings, which are drawn overwhelmingly from

the words of Second Isaiah, with the result that
the specific emphases of the original Isaiah are
often missed.

Beyond these three foci is an insistence on the importance of an altogether different matter: the way texts in
Isaiah functioned for Jews as well as for Christians. This
is the subject matter of Chapter 7. Thus it may be a surprise to Christians that the traditional Jewish *haftarot*
readings from Isaiah for Sabbaths and feast-days are taken
just as overwhelmingly from chapters 40–66 as Christian
lectionary readings are. Now I do not expect that this work
will be as useful for Jewish study groups as for Christian
ones, but at least I hope I have not distorted Jewish sen-
sibilities in what I present. While Christians and Jews differ in the placement Isaiah in their respective
proclamations, Christians need nevertheless to deepen an
appreciation of the ways Jews share with them the book
of Isaiah, and indeed an awareness that the book was the
possession of Jews long before the emergence of Christian communities (the need for this awareness is under-
lined by the first illustration I offer in Chapter 1). Many
Christians are often surprised that there even *is* a Jewish
sensibility about Isaiah. Norman Podhoretz, a leading
American Jewish intellectual, in writing about the book
of Isaiah, after mentioning the obscurity of much of the
book, has this to say:

> And there is yet another factor that deepens the prob-
> lem of discovering what the book of Isaiah has to say
> to us today. This consists of the selective readings and
> outright misrepresentations to which the text has been
> subjected by three different groups to whom Isaiah is
> a special favorite: Reform Jews, political liberals, and
> Christians.[12]

Clearly there are other vantage points from which to view the book of Isaiah than Christian ones. In any event I hope that this book will encourage the reader to look beyond the specific selections heard in the course of worship to the book of Isaiah itself, to look at the lines both before and after those selections, to be alert to the contexts of the selections, and in general to make the acquaintance of one of the most astonishing books of Scripture.

Occasionally there is a difference of versification between Protestant Bibles on the one hand and Jewish and Roman Catholic Bibles on the other: the former refers to Isaiah 9:2–7 while the latter numbers these verses as 1–6. In this work I follow the former versification.

The following works have been particularly helpful to me in the preparation of this work: Hans Wildberger, *Isaiah 1–12*, *Isaiah 13–27*, and *Jesaja 28–39*;[13] Ronald E. Clements, *Isaiah 1–39*;[14] H. G. M. Williamson, *The Book Called Isaiah*;[15] Walter Brueggemann, *Isaiah 40–66*;[16] the various articles in the collection Craig C. Broyles and Craig A. Evans, *Writing and Reading the Scroll of Isaiah, Studies of an Interpretive Tradition*,[17] and Brevard S. Childs, *Isaiah*.[18]

I should like here to express appreciation to Professor Childs for allowing me to read proof pages of his commentary on Isaiah before its publication; and to Gordon W. Lathrop, Charles A. Schieren Professor of Liturgy, the Lutheran Theological Seminary at Philadelphia, and to Horace T. Allen, Jr., Associate Professor of Worship, Boston University School of Theology, for advice and help on various details.

NOTES ON THE LECTIONARIES

Many readers will have some idea of how a lectionary works, especially if they are accustomed to hearing readings Sunday by Sunday from a particular lectionary. Nevertheless it may be useful to offer an outline here of what is involved.

A *lectionary* is a book of lections (i.e, "lessons"or Scripture readings), or a list of the Scriptures to be read throughout the Christian church year, or a sequence of church years. These are appointed or, in some instances, commended by a given church body for use in its liturgies (i.e., worship services). Primary in importance are the lectionaries that set forth the lections for Sundays and the major festivals. Beyond these lectionaries for Sundays and the major festivals, there are also daily lectionaries, specifically the Roman Catholic Weekday Lectionary for daily Masses. Though there is also a daily eucharistic lectionary used by some monastic orders in the Anglican (Episcopal) tradition, by the occasional congregations that maintain weekday services, and by those who use these readings in their homes, it is fair to say that this lectionary plays a much smaller role in the sensibility of Episcopalians than does the weekday lectionary for Roman Catholics.

The Roman Catholic lectionaries evolved through the centuries. Then, as a consequence of the Second Vatican Council, they were revised (and, in particular, greatly enriched by more Old Testament texts) and published in 1969.[19] The various Lutheran churches and the Episcopal Church in the United States and Anglican Church in Canada rather quickly adopted lectionaries for Sundays and the major festivals that were close to those used by Roman Catholics (Lutherans in 1978 and Episcopalians in 1979[20]).

Meanwhile, in the context of this process, beginning in the 1960s, a remarkable development emerged in the United States and Canada, with later parallel developments in other English-speaking areas: a Consultation on Common Texts was formed by various Protestant figures, especially those from the Presbyterian and Methodist Churches and from the United Church of Christ and the Christian Churches (Disciples of Christ), meeting with Lutherans, Episcopalians, and Roman Catholics. The result of that group's work has been the Common Lectionary (now the Revised Common Lectionary). This lectionary has been commended to Christian churches that do not already maintain a lectionary.[21] Further, the Evangelical Lutheran Church in America, which had maintained a lectionary of its own, has now adopted with few variations the selection of readings of the Revised Common Lectionary; and the Episcopalian lectionary conforms to it to a great degree, so that the readings for Sundays and the major festivals, in particular, have come to essential conformity. (Unfortunately, however, there is still some lack of uniformity in the nomenclature for a given Sunday, as I shall explain below.)

The church year begins with the First Sunday of Advent (the fourth Sunday before December 25), at the earliest, November 27 and at the latest December 3. The lectionaries for Sundays and the major festivals are arranged in a three-year cycle (Years A, B, and C). Year A begins on the First Sunday of Advent in any calendar year which is divisible by three without a remainder. Thus, since 2001 is divisible by 3 without a remainder, Year A began on December 2, 2001. Year B then began on December 1, 2002. Year C on November 30, 2003, and so forth.

The lectionaries for Sundays and the major festivals set forth for each occasion three lessons and after the first lesson, a response. The first lesson is taken from the Old Testament (or, in the Easter season, the of Acts of the Apostles),[22] the second from the New Testament epistles (or the Revelation to John), and the third from the gospels. The response after the first lesson is usually a psalm or portion of a psalm. Inasmuch as the topic of the present work is the book of Isaiah, I will say nothing in regard to the responses or epistle lessons, and in regard to the gospel lessons only that the gospel during Year A is largely Matthew, during Year B Mark, and in Year C Luke, while on certain Sundays, notably during the later Sundays during Lent and during the Easter season, John is read.

The Weekday Lectionary of the Roman Catholic Church follows an independent two-year cycle (designated Years I and II). Year I begins with the season of Advent preceding an odd-numbered year; thus one has the beginning of Year I on December 1, 2002, and November 28, 2004, and of Year II on November 30, 2003, and November 27, 2005. In this lectionary there are two readings rather than three. The second reading is always from the gospels, while the first reading is either from the Old Testament, the epistles, Acts or Revelation, and again there is a response, usually from a psalm, after the first reading.

Advent is followed in the church year by the Christmas season. The Christmas season is closed by the Epiphany (January 6), which in some traditions, may be observed on the Sunday immediately preceding or following (the Sunday between January 2 and 8) The lectionaries offer fixed readings for Lent and the Easter season, but, given the fact that the date of Easter can vary between March 22 and April 25, and consequently that Ash Wednesday can vary between February 4 and March 10 and Pentecost between May 10 and June 13, the number of Sundays between the first Sunday after Epiphany and Ash Wednesday can be as few as three and as many as nine, and the number of Sundays after Pentecost (through the remainder of a given church year) varies correspondingly.

Roman Catholics designate by the perhaps unfortu-
nate term "Ordinary Time" the period beginning with the
first Monday within January 8–14 and ending with the
Tuesday just before Ash Wednesday, and again beginning
with the Sunday after Pentecost (Trinity Sunday) and
ending with the Saturday just before the first Sunday of
Advent. Since it is always Sunday that is reckoned to be
the first day of the week, and since Ordinary Time begins
on a Monday, the sequence of *Sundays* in Ordinary Time
begins in January with the *Second* Sunday in Ordinary
Time (it is the Sunday that falls between January 14 and
20); the Last (Thirty-fourth) Sunday in Ordinary Time, the
Sunday in November before Advent begins, is designated
the Solemnity of Christ the King (it is the Sunday between
November 20 and 26).

The Revised Common Lectionary avoids the term
Ordinary Time and instead simply designates a given Sunday within a seven-day compass of the calendar year—for
example, "Sunday Between January 21 and 27," and this
neutral designation has in general been adopted by Episcopalians and Lutherans as well. But there are complications in the designations of given Sundays by
Episcopalians and Lutherans (and for this reason the
reader may want to skip the balance of this paragraph!).
Episcopalians prefer to reckon the Sundays after the
Epiphany and before Lent by numerical order ("Third
Sunday After the Epiphany"); furthermore, for Sundays on
or after February 11 until the last Sunday before Lent, and
for all the Sundays after Pentecost, Episcopalians and
Lutherans number the sequence of "Propers" (i.e., the set
of lections belonging to a given Sunday), a sequence
which is always five less than the number of a given Sunday in the Roman Catholic reckoning of Ordinary Time.
For example, the Sunday between February 11 and 17 is
reckoned by Roman Catholics as the Sixth Sunday in

Ordinary Time, while Episcopalians and Lutherans speak
of the readings of that Sunday as "Proper 1." And for
Lutherans, though they continue to hold to the designation of Sundays after Pentecost by the old style of reckoning ("the Tenth Sunday After Pentecost"), *the actual
readings* are no longer tied to that title but rather conform
to the system of the Revised Common Lectionary tied to
the secular calendar, already explained ("the Sunday
Between July 24 and 30").

It is my hope that these notes will help the reader to
make sense out of the references to various readings in
the present work. I shall confine these references to the
system used in the Revised Common Lectionary. Thus
when discussing Isaiah 49:1–7, I shall indicate that it is
the first reading for the Sunday between January 14 and
20 in Year A.

It is also to be noted that for Roman Catholics the
liturgy of the hours (morning and evening prayer) during
Ordinary Time is set forth in a four-week cycle of readings and prayers. More specific readings and prayers are
appointed for the seasons of Advent, Christmas, Lent,
and Easter. Beyond various prayer sentences and hymns,
this liturgy consists of psalms and canticles (hymn-like
passages drawn from other biblical or extra-biblical
sources).

NOTES

1. William L. Holladay, *Isaiah, Scroll of a Prophetic Heritage*
(Grand Rapids MI: Eerdmans, 1978; repr. New York: Pilgrim,
1987).

2. William L. Holladay, *The Psalms Through Three Thousand
Years: Prayerbook for a Cloud of Witnesses* (Minneapolis: Fortress,
1993).

3. William L. Holladay, *Long Ago God Spoke: How Christians May
Hear the Old Testament Today* (Minneapolis: Fortress, 1995).

4. Peter C. Bower (ed.), *Handbook for the Revised Common Lectionary* (Louisville: Westminister John Knox, 1996).

5. *The Book of Common Prayer* (New York: The Church Hymnal Corporation, 1979).

6. *The Vatican II Sunday Missal* (Boston: Daughters of St. Paul, 1974).

7. In this work I shall take note of Lutheran readings only when they diverge from those of the Revised Common Lectionary. For the Lutheran readings see now *Indexes for Worship Planning* (Minneapolis: Augsburg, 1996). It is to be stressed that in general the congregations of the Evangelical Lutheran Church in America no longer follow the lectionary readings published in the *Lutheran Book of Worship* (Minneapolis: Augsburg, 1978).

8. *The Vatican Weekday Missal* (Boston: Daughters of St. Paul, 1975).

9. *Christian Prayer: The Liturgy of the Hours* (Boston: Daughters of St. Paul, 1974).

10. In this work I use the abbreviations BCE, "before Common Era," and CE, "Common Era," for the traditional abreviations BC and AD, respectively.

11. H. G. M. Williamson, *The Book Called Isaiah: Deutero-Isaiah's Role in Composition and Redaction* (Oxford: Clarendon, 1994).

12. Norman Podhoretz, "Learning from Isaiah," *Commentary* 109, no.5 (May 2000): 32.

13. Hans Wildberger, *Isaiah 1–12* (German original 1980; English transl.: Continental Commentaries; Minneapolis: Fortress Press, 1991); Isaiah 13–27 (German original 1978; English transl.: Continental Commentaries; Minneapolis: Fortress Press, 1997); *Jesaja 28–39* (Biblischer Kommentar, Altes Testament, X/3; Neukirchen: Neukirchener Verlag, 1982).

14. Ronald E. Clements, *Isaiah 1–39* (The New Century Bible Commentary; London: Marshall, Morgan & Scott, Grand Rapids, MI.: Eerdmans, 1980).

15. H. G. M. Williamson, *The Book Called Isaiah: Deutero-Isaiah's Role in Composition and Redaction* (Oxford: Clarendon, 1994).

16. Walter Brueggemann, *Isaiah 40–66* (Westminster Bible Companion; Louisville, KY: Westminster John Knox, 1998).

17. Craig C. Broyles and Craig A. Evans (eds.), *Writing and Reading the Scroll of Isaiah: Studies of an Interpretive Tradition* (Supplements to Vetus Testamentum 70; Leiden: Brill, 1997).

18. Brevard S. Childs, *Isaiah* (Old Testament Library; Louisville, KY: Westminster John Knox, 2001).

19. For details see Clifford Howell, "From Trent to Vatican II," in Cheslyn Jones, Geoffrey Wainwright, and Edward Yarnold (eds.), *The Study of Liturgy* (New York: Oxford University Press, 1978).

20. See notes 6 and 8.

21. Horace T. Allen, Jr., "Introduction: Preaching in a Christian Context," in Peter C. Bower (ed.), *Handbook for the Revised Common Lectionary* (Louisville: Westminster John Knox, 1996), 1–24.

22. In the Episcopal lectionary during Easter the first lesson may be taken either from the Old Testament or Acts

Chapter 1

"Isaiah 'Twas Foretold It": Three Ways to Hear a Prophet

DURING THE COFFEE BREAK of the first session of an evening course on Isaiah in a local church, a woman approached me with a curious combination of urgency and furtiveness—clearly she was puzzled by what I had presented. "I have just one question," she said. I nodded. "Was Isaiah a Jew?" she asked. Alas, my urge to tease got the better of me. "Let me tell you," I answered, "not only was Isaiah a Jew, but all the kings he spoke to were Jews too." "Oh," she replied with a sharp intake of breath, "I had no idea."

There was no chance then or later to confront what I took to be anti-Semitism implied in her query, but the encounter has remained with me through the years. For too many Christians, the book of Isaiah remains only a unique mine of proof texts to be drawn upon, particularly during Advent and Lent. Indeed we appear have made the prophet Isaiah an honorary Christian! So when, if ever, we meet Isaiah in his own historical context, in Judah in the eighth century BCE, we are often disoriented.

Let me offer another incident, this time from an introductory undergraduate class in the Old Testament that I was teaching in a Midwestern college. My lectures attempted to put Old Testament passages into their original historical context, those of Isaiah included, and among those I had dealt with was Isaiah 9:2–7 ("For unto us a child is born"). I laid out the general conclusion of scholars: that Isaiah originally spoke these words as an ode on the occasion in Judah perhaps of the birth of a royal child, or more likely, of the crowning of a new king, such as Hezekiah (I shall return to this text in Chapter 3). Then, as it happened, I was asked to read the Old Testament lesson for Christmas Eve at a pre-Christmas-break vesper service. That lesson was Isaiah. 9:2, 6–7. The next afternoon, in the Old Testament class, one of the brighter students accused me: "You finked out last night," he said. "Here in class you taught us what the passage was all about, and then you went ahead and used it just the way the church has always done."

I cannot recall now all the details of my answer to his challenge, but clearly this question of what a text *meant* and what it *is now taken to mean*, indeed the legitimacy of any specific Christian uses of Old Testament texts, is a steady and urgent question for thoughtful Bible readers. To clarify what is at stake we need to examine three ways to hear these old texts.

ISAIAH WAS SPEAKING ABOUT US

We begin with what the Church has traditionally done with Old Testament texts, exemplified by the lines beginning the second stanza of the Christmas hymn, "Lo, how a Rose e'er blooming": "Isaiah 'twas foretold it, the Rose I have in mind." In this understanding, there are various Old Testament texts that speak of the coming of Jesus Christ and of events in his life and the life of the early Church. Christians have found in Isaiah, in the psalms, and in other Old Testament books predictions and anticipations of the gospel story, and this is how Christians have heard (and still hear) the texts.

Now it must be affirmed at the outset that when Christians do this, they are doing just what the New Testament itself does. The New Testament writers, particularly Matthew, draw on a whole array of Old Testament passages with remarks like, "This was to fulfill what had been spoken through the prophet" (see Matthew 1:22; 2:15; 8:17; 12:17; 13:35; 21:4). By this understanding the prophets predicted what was to them the future, the Christian future.

Indeed this is what Jesus himself is remembered as having done. In Luke 4:16–21 the story is told of Jesus' attendance at the synagogue in Nazareth. He asked for the scroll of Isaiah, read from it Isaiah 61:1–2, and then said, "Today this scripture has been fulfilled in your hearing." And for hosts of Christian believers through the centuries, such testimony was and is today utterly convincing: if the New Testament understands Old Testament texts this way, if Jesus himself understood Old Testament texts this way, then this is the way God intends *us* to understand them. The rationale is elegant, tight, and much too simple.

Thoughtful people will realize that within this mode of understanding serious questions arise almost immediately. For example, one may ask what "fulfill" really means. Indeed it may be useful to pause and ponder this matter for a moment. Originally the Hebrew word for "fill" was used when previously announced *words* were strengthened and actualized by a subsequent *event*. Thus in 1 Kings 8:15 Solomon announces that God with his hand has "fulfilled" (literally "filled") what he had promised with his mouth through the prophet Nathan to David. This Hebrew idiom passed over into the Greek translation of the Old Testament (the Septuagint) and was therefore available to the New Testament writers.

But as we think about it, we realize that all kinds of pronouncements are capable of being "fulfilled." Thus, most simply, a prophet may make a prediction about the future, and a later generation may see that prediction occur in the way the prophet had in mind. Or, again, a prophet may make a prediction about the future, but he may have in mind his own near future, while centuries later a fresh generation becomes convinced that the words really refer to their own time. Or, again, a prophet may make, not a prediction, but a statement about his own present which a generation centuries later is convinced really refers to their own circumstances. Whatever the relation between the original intention and the later understanding of fulfilment, the important thing to bear in mind about this way of understanding Old Testament texts is the emphasis on what the later generation understands is *really* what the text means.

Now there are several consequences to this understanding. It stresses the eternal purpose of God in the text—this is what is primary: in this mode of understanding, the prophet is simply a passive channel for God's communication. Thus little or no attention is paid to what the prophet may consciously have had in mind when the text is first proclaimed, or to what his first hearers may take the text to mean. At its crudest, this understanding conjures up a vision of a prophet speaking out a word which he does not understand, or at least does not fully understand, to an audience of folk who do not understand it either, or at least not fully. The notion of a prophet scratching his head in puzzlement before an equally puzzled audience is disturbing.

Furthermore, by this mode of reading no alternative understanding of the text is possible. In particular, Christians reading a text beloved to them will reject the validity of any Jewish understanding of that text. The only valid interpretation of the text is the Christian one. Those who know some history will immediately think of medieval the disputations between Jews and Christians over what particular texts mean. These encounters between Jews and Christians were rarely edifying and remain dark chapters in our shared history.[1]

Speaking of history, there is a further detail to be noted in regard to this mode of reading Old Testament texts, and that is that *every* faith community that has drawn on the Old Testament has had this same understanding of the way to use such texts—the Dead Sea Scroll community, for example. The Dead Sea Scrolls, as is well known, were copied and preserved by a Jewish sect during two centuries around Jesus' time, and among the scrolls is a commentary on the book of Habakkuk, a prophet who lived late in the seventh century BCE. This commentary consists a sequence of passages of Habakkuk, usually one or two verses, each followed by the expression, "Its interpretation: . . ." The interpretations steadily relate to the life and times *of the sect.* For example, the commentary cites Habbakkuk. 1:4, "And justice never prevails; the wicked surround the righteous," and follows it with, "Its interpretation: the wicked is the Wicked Priest and the righteous is the Teacher of Righteousness."[2] The "Teacher of Righteousness" is the designation given to the founder of the sect (about 150 BCE), and the "Wicked Priest" is evidently an authority of that time in Jerusalem who persecuted the founder. (There are also among the Dead Sea Scrolls commentaries on passages in the book of Isaiah, but unfortunately that material has survived only in scraps.[3])

Another document among the Dead Sea Scrolls consists of a chain of citations from the Old Testament that served as "proof texts." What is left of this document contains citations from 2 Samuel 7:10–14 and Psalm 2, among other passages.[4] Alert Christians will recall that the first chapter of the letter to the Hebrews in the New Testament contains citations from those very same passages (see Hebrews 1.5). But whereas in Hebrews the citations are understood to refer to *Jesus Christ,* in the Dead Sea document the passages are understood to refer to the events in the last days described by their own doctrine. The Dead Sea sect, then, was doing precisely what the writers and readers of the New Testament were doing— finding in passages of the Old Testament various references to their own belief system.

Nevertheless, as I stated at the outset, this mode of reading, that these texts refer to details in our Christian story, is the traditional reading of these texts by the Church. It need hardly be said, this mode of reading continues today to sustain the faith of millions of Christians, not only of those who hold to the "infallibility" of Scripture but of also the faith of hosts of other Bible readers both inside and outside various Christian churches. This mode of reading develops when two circumstances prevail: when readers understand the texts to be given by God, and when at the same time they are not aware of the time-boundedness of these texts—not aware of the original historical circumstances—or at least do not take account of these.

Indeed it is a way of reading that *all* Christians fall into from time to time, no matter how much history one has learned, because there is no end to the history one has yet to learn. Nevertheless it is an insufficient way of reading the text, so we will not dwell on it in this study. Instead, we are invited to consider the original circumstances of the texts, and so we turn to the second way of hearing them.

THE TEXTS OF ISAIAH WERE SPEAKING TO THEIR OWN GENERATION

In this second mode of hearing the texts, we begin with the assumption that, in common with all the passages of the Old Testament, the texts of Isaiah are *time-bound*—that is to say, when each of them was first proclaimed, it was in the context of a particular historical circumstance. Further, one takes for granted that a given proclamation carried meaning for the prophet and was heard with approximately the same meaning by those in the audience. Once these assumptions are stated, it is easy to grasp them; but, as a matter of fact, it is only in the last couple of hundred years, with the emergence of what has come to be called "the historical-critical method," that scholars have been able to open effectively to ordinary readers of the Bible the details of those historical circumstances and those sets of meanings (this is what I presented to the evening course on Isaiah, and what I set forth in the Introduction to the Old Testament class).

I say, "It is easy to grasp them," but the historical details bring a shock of pleased surprise to many of the folk who are exposed to the method. In a congregation in which I provided leadership some years ago, I formed the habit of offering a short introduction before a Scripture reading in Sunday morning worship, something like this: "The Old Testament lesson this morning is Isaiah 40:1–8. This passage was spoken by the prophet at the end of the period of Jewish exile in Babylon, when the great question was when they would be allowed to return to Jerusalem." After a few months of this, a deacon of the church came to me and said, "You know, I've begun to realize something I never knew before—that Scripture texts have a context." Here was a man who had been reading the Bible thoughtfully for his entire adult life, for whom this was a fresh notion.

Again there is a common reaction that I hear from people who are exposed to some of the fruits of this scholarly endeavor in the Old Testament material that I offer in lay courses, namely, "You make the Bible come alive." It is frightening, of course, to think of what the Bible was like before it came alive (that much of it was dead!), but of course for too many Christians the Old Testament, at least, resembles a vast swamp of puzzling and largely unread passages punctuated by a few texts heavy with Christian import. They blink and stand amazed when a whole set of searchlights suddenly illuminates the landscape.

One learns, for example, that the Old Testament prophets were not primarily in the business of predicting the far future but rather understood themselves to be called by God to diagnose the predicaments of their own generation, particularly in times of national emergency. They offered plausible outcomes for their people, depending on whether the people responded to God or not. One learns also that circles of followers, disciples perhaps, of a given prophet, being convinced without question that God had spoken through their master, collected his words for themselves and for later generations.

Now in order to make the Bible come alive one has to gain some kind of understanding of the history and thought-world of these various people from far away and long ago. It is not easy to come by the array of details needed for this task. I shall offer some of these details in the course of this book, though I hope with a light touch. This second way of reading the texts may appear to be liberating, but it brings consequences and complications in its wake. Let me mention a few.

The first is that it approaches the Old Testament, in our case the book of Isaiah, with the tools one would bring to bear on any human text from the past. As a parallel, suppose we were reading a passage from Dante's *Inferno*. Now whether we are reading the passage in the original Italian or in some English translation, we will benefit immensely if we know something about those popes were who are assigned to the various levels of hell. If we are reading the passage in the original Italian, we will want to be sure we have a good grip on Dante's vocabulary of the early fourteenth century, and we will pay attention to his artistic use of the intricate rhyme-scheme of *terza rima*.

The historical-critical method approaches texts from Isaiah in precisely the same way. We seek to understand the nature of the Assyrian threat to the kingdom of Judah in the eighth century BCE, and we draw on whatever expertise we can find to understand Isaiah's skill in Hebrew poetic forms. We must grasp Isaiah's assumptions about God that he shared with his fellow-citizens, about his notions of covenant, of kingship, and all the rest. Above all, we need to understand the assumptions that Isaiah and his hearers shared regarding the role of a prophet as one who speaks for God.

There is another crucial matter in connection with the book of Isaiah: scholars have concluded that chapters

40–66 of the book are not to be attributed to the original Isaiah at all, but to one or more nameless prophets who lived two centuries later (this is the "Second Isaiah" I mention in the Introduction). This is to say, the book of Isaiah–unlike Dante's *Divine Comedy*–but like many other biblical books, is a compilation that has a complicated literary history of its own. Those who espouse the historical-critical method must grapple with the idea that the book of Isaiah offers the words of more than one prophet, and that one must find the historical circumstances of Isaiah 40 and following, not in the eighth century BCE at all, but in the quite different circumstances of the sixth century BCE.

Now to those who take it without question that the books of the prophets are God's word through those specific named prophets, this idea is profoundly disturbing. It shakes their whole understanding of the Bible. One of my students once came to me troubled by just this issue. He had indeed followed my analysis of the sixth-century historical context for chapters 40 and beyond. "But why," he asked, "if Methuselah lived for 969 years, could Isaiah not have lived for 220 years?" It was a line of thought I had never encountered before, and one for which, I admit, I had no ready answer, not wishing to complicate things for him even further by raising the question of the historicity of Methuselah.

But if one brings to bear on the texts of Isaiah the same assumptions not only about the normal span of human life but about the human condition that one employs with any other text from the past, then one assumes that whatever else these texts are, they are certainly products of human beings. They are therefore susceptible to analysis as are other ancient texts. Even though we may well understand the texts as in some sense attributable to God, we do not assume that God shields them from the normal human shaping that any text undergoes. In fact we can go on to say that it is possible for a scholar to do useful work on texts from Isaiah even if he or she does not have an active belief in God. Indeed one can go further still and admit that it would be possible to do useful work on texts from Isaiah even if it should turn out that God does not exist. How could this be? Because what Isaiah thought and proclaimed out of his own belief system might be profoundly relevant to the human condition in both his day and ours. Now as it happens, I am a Christian, and I speak out of the community of Christians and out of the belief in God that is shared in that community. But the *method* of working on texts of Isaiah does not depend upon the theological beliefs of those who work on the texts. So I repeat, we do not assume that God exempts biblical texts from the normal human shaping that any other text undergoes. This is a crucial point to which we shall return.

One could summarize our discussion up to this point by saying that the first way to read the texts assumes that God intends an eternal, unequivocal meaning to biblical texts once and for all, and the prophetic purveyors of the texts, in our instance Isaiah, are passive channels for that divine meaning. The second way to read the texts assumes the existence of steady shifting in historical circumstances and in the outlook of those who live through those circumstances. In this way of reading the texts the individual prophets come to the fore. It is they on whom the spotlight shines.

But this way of hearing the old texts brings with it a huge problem, obviously. If the texts were originally destined for folk who are far away and long ago, then what are *we* expected to hear in the texts? Are the old texts of purely antiquarian value, like Greek myths, offering a variety of specifics in the lives of our spiritual ancestors, or do they–can they–speak to us in our day? And if so, how are we supposed to hear them? This is, of course, the question that the student in my class was raising when he accused me of finking out when reading Isaiah 9 as a text for Christmas Eve. Ultimately the question is what God intends us to hear in the texts. And so we turn to the third way of hearing the text.

NOW WE REALLY KNOW WHAT ISAIAH MEANS!

I was a soldier in the American army stationed in northern Italy in January 1947. Our base was near Leghorn (Livorno), and I was out on a pass, hitchhiking to Florence. It was a bitterly cold winter day, and in those months just after the end of the Second World War there was little public transportation. A gasoline truck stopped to pick me up, and in the cab, beside the driver, there was already a young Italian nun whom the driver had picked up before he stopped for me. By then I had learned to speak a bit of Italian, and the two of us passengers struck up a conversation with each other. What sort of job did I do in the army, she wanted to know. "I am assistant to the Protestant chaplain," I explained. "You are a *Protestant?*" she asked with some alarm—I was doubtless the first such person she had ever encountered, and for all I know she may have been surprised that I did not have horns. "Yes," I admitted, "I am Protestant." "But are you baptized?" she persisted. "Yes," I assured her. It was an act that had been done at the behest of my parents in a Presbyterian church in southern California on Easter Sunday when I was not quite two years old. "But if you were baptized," she persisted, "why were you not baptized in the true faith?" An unbaptized pagan she could grasp, but if the act is to be done at all, why not do it right? At this point I lost my grip. "Sister," I said, "it is difficult for me to explain in English, and impossible in Italian." And that is where we left that ecumenical encounter.

Now this incident from 1947 became in later years a family joke. I returned from the army and finished my undergraduate degree, went on to seminary, and was ordained into the United Church of Christ. Occasionally my parents and I recalled the nun's naïveté, and someone would remark on my parents' neglect in getting me "baptized in the true faith." But then on Easter Eve of 1985, through a variety of personal circumstances far too intricate to relate here, I entered the Roman Catholic Church, of all things, at which point I reverted to lay status. Now, one may ask, what is the *real* meaning of that conversation in the Italian gas truck? Was my eventual conversion to the Catholic faith the result of the fervent prayers of that nun during the intervening thirty-eight years? I have always been convinced that God has a wild sense of humor, and while admittedly I raise the question of the nun's prayers partly tongue-in-cheek, certainly many people do have the experience of looking back at a memorable event in earlier years and saying, "Now I *really* know what God intended for me [when I lost that job, when I got married, when my mother died, or whatever]." The nun's question in the gas truck, and my shift in churchly identity decades later, at least throw into relief the theological questions I am raising now, of the *real* meaning of a text.

The third way of hearing a text is to open ourselves to the possibility of *multiple* real meanings. That is to say, we can become acquainted with what a text of Isaiah meant to the prophet himself and to his hearers. We can

also discern what the same text later came to mean to subsequent generations of believers, including generations of
Christians—yes, including ourselves. And most crucially,
we can discern the legitimacy of more than a single understanding of the text—indeed we can discern the intentionality of God in more than a single understanding of
the text.

This is not a modern idea. Four and a half centuries
ago John Calvin was commenting on Isaiah 61:1, part of
the passage which, as we have seen, Jesus is remembered
as having applied to himself in the synagogue in Nazareth.
Calvin wrote,

> As Christ explains this passage with reference to him-
> self (Luke 4:18), so commentators limit it to him with-
> out hesitation, and lay down this principle, that Christ
> is introduced as speaking, as if the whole passage
> related to him alone. The Jews laugh at this, as an ill-
> advised application to Christ of that which is equally
> applicable to other prophets. My opinion is, that this
> chapter is added as a seal to the former [that is, chap-
> ter 60], to confirm what had hitherto been said about
> restoring the Church of Christ [that is, the nation of
> Israel]; and that for this purpose Christ testifies that
> he has been anointed by God, in consequence of
> which he justly applies this prophecy to himself; for
> he has exhibited clearly and openly what others have
> laid down in an obscure manner. But this is not incon-
> sistent with the application of this statement to other
> prophets, whom the Lord has anointed; . . .

It is a subtle argument: *both* Isaiah *and* Christ, not at all
the either/or position which too many Christians take. We
shall return to this text in Chapter 6, and to Calvin in
Chapter 8.

Three decades ago the Old Testament scholar Phyllis Trible described the matter this way: "All scripture is

a pilgrim, wandering through history, engaging in new settings, and ever refusing to be locked in the box of the past."[5] In this understanding, the "box of the past" is the original setting of Isaiah, but the text has a life of its own and will not be confined to that original setting. I would put it somewhat differently—I would say that God speaks through the old text in fresh ways in fresh settings.

Let me then shift the image a bit. The old texts are like old reel-to-reel tapes we find in a cupboard or closet. We play the tapes. They are scratchy, for the recording techniques when they were made were not the best, but there they are, old songs and stories. At first we are not sure who many of those people are who figure in the songs and stories, Uncle Albert and Cousin Minnie and the rest. We realize right away that the tapes were not prepared with us in mind at all but for the families and friends of those who made the tapes in the first place. In a way we are eavesdroppers on the old tapes. This is what we are today with respect to Old Testament texts—eavesdroppers on old tapes. But—and I hasten to add the crucial point—God *intends* us to be eavesdroppers. "Here," God says to us, "listen to these old tapes. They are filled with my conversation with biblical Israel. Learn how they dealt with me and above all how I dealt with them. Then, with these tapes ringing in your ears, I invite you to your own specific conversations with me."

At first this approach seems scary and confusing; we like things to stay simple. These things do not seem to be altogether simple. I suspect that this way to think about the meaning of the texts is closer to what the texts ask of us than either of the first two ways to hear them. But, as with the first two ways, this method brings problems with it too. I see two crucial ones. The first is this: How are we to understand the old texts responsibly? Since of the

devising of presumed meanings for biblical texts there can
be no end. There is always a steady stream of anecdotes
and jokes in Christian circles regarding bizarre interpretations of biblical passages, like the one about the pastor,
a sworn enemy of alcoholic beverages, who was able to
persuade himself and his congregation that 1 Timothy
5:23 ("Take a little wine for the sake of your stomach.")
was a reference to a liniment to be rubbed on the surface
of the skin. So I repeat: how are we to understand the old
texts responsibly?

I see no way to make rules about this beforehand.
Each generation, faced with fresh questions that demand
theological scrutiny, will hear the old texts with fresh ears.
Thus, to offer a current example, in our generation the
claims of women are being heard with fresh urgency, so
that we hear Isaiah 49:14–18, a passage in which the
prophet, speaking for God, offers a comparison between
God and a mother concerned for her nursing child, with
our ears alert to this application of feminine language and
imagery. I think we must simply examine our texts one by
one, and work through them with theological integrity.
This is what we shall try to do in the following chapters
of this work.

The second problem we face with this mode of understanding the texts is: How are we to deal with interpretations other than our own? About twenty years ago I was
asked to address a mixed group of pastors and rabbis on
the topic of how our faith communities might proclaim
Isaiah 53. This is the passage, "He was despised and
rejected of men," the Old Testament lesson that Christians have traditionally used on Good Friday. For me, as
for Philip in Acts 8, this passage is central for Christian
proclamation. No other Old Testament passage is so crucial for my faith. And yet it is heavy with meaning for Jew-

ish communities as well, communities that in no way see in its lines any description of Jesus Christ. My presentation to the pastors and rabbis that day stretched to the limit my ability to affirm the integrity of multiple meanings in the texts of Scripture.

With these matters in mind we now turn to the book of Isaiah.

NOTES

1. Readers who want some details can refer to the chapter on the twelfth-century Andrew of St. Victor in Beryl Smalley, *The Study of the Bible in the Middle Ages* (Oxford: Blackwell, 1952; repr. Notre Dame, IN: University of Notre Dame Press, 1964). Check also William Horbury, *Christianity in Ancient Jewish Tradition, Inaugural Lecture Delivered at the University of Cambridge, 4 February 1999* (Cambridge: Cambridge University Press, 2000).

2. The document is called 1QpHab; see Florentino García Martínez, *The Dead Sea Scrolls Translated* (trans. Wilfred G.E. Watson; Leiden,: E.J. Brill, 1994), 198.

3. Ibid., 185–91.

4. The document is now called 4QFlorilegium or 4Q174; see ibid., 136.

5. Phyllis Trible, "Ancient Priests and Modern Polluters," *Andover Newton Quarterly* 12/2

Chapter 2 ————————————

God Is High and Holy,
And Israel Is Disobedient

WHAT DO WE KNOW about the original Isaiah? As to biographical details, we have, alas, almost no information about him at all. We have no dates or accounts of his birth or death. The secure biographical information we do have about him I shall offer in the balance of this paragraph. He was called to be a prophet in the year 742 BCE. in an overwhelming vision of God (Isaiah 6:1). He was married, though we do not know his wife's name—she is simply referred to as "the prophetess" (8:3). He gave two sons strange, symbolic names, Shear-jashub (7:3) and Maher-shalal-hash-baz (8:3). There are the details of an encounter with the young King Ahaz, evidently in 734 BCE (7:1–17). He had disciples (8:16). That is really all.

Beyond these few details, we have narratives in 2 Kings 19–20 of his dealings with King Hezekiah at the time of the siege of Jerusalem by the Assyrian king Sennacherib in the year 701. This material is repeated in Isaiah 36–39 with some additions. But many scholars suspect that these historical reminiscences were collected a century after his death, so that it is difficult to be sure of their historical core.[1]

This dearth of biographical material is a good example of the lack of purely "human interest" material in the Old Testament. What many of us are curious about are the personalities of the Bible. Unfortunately the Old Testament does not give us what we crave—it cares about a different matter altogether, namely words from God. Accordingly the book of Isaiah offers us words about which this claim is made, leaving it for us to glean any details we can, indeed any surmises we can, regarding the prophet's life and personality.

If we lack biographical facts about him, what can we know about his message? A great deal. However, the material we have, all within chapters 1–39, comes in short spurts, and not only are those spurts not in chronological order, but they are often without any clear indications of beginnings and ends. Indeed they are sometimes rearranged, we suspect, from their original order, and intermixed, we also suspect, with a great deal of material that is not from Isaiah but from disciples who lived decades and even centuries after his time. The first thirty-nine chapters of the book of Isaiah represent an immense scrapbook, the ordering process of which is not always clear.

Christians who wish to become acquainted with the prophet's message face a further barrier if they depend on lectionary readings heard in church. Lectionary readings that stem from the original Isaiah do not give a balanced account of his message. What I shall do in this chapter and the next, then, is to introduce Isaiah's message, using lectionary readings when possible. I will do this under four points:

- God is high and holy, but Israel is disobedient
- God's people Israel have broken the norms of the covenant;
- God is bringing Assyria upon the nation as a punishment;
- ultimately there is hope for Israel's future in a purified Jerusalem and a purified kingship.

The first two points I shall take up in this chapter, and the second two in Chapter 3.

GOD IS HIGH AND HOLY, BUT ISRAEL IS DISOBEDIENT

The best way to approach these topics is to examine chapter 6 of Isaiah, the prophet's report of his original vision of God. I omit the last verse, v. 13, which is utterly obscure in the original Hebrew.

(1)   In the year that King Uzziah died, I saw the Lord sitting on a throne, high and lofty; and the hem of his robe filled the temple. (2) Seraphs were in attendance above him; each had six wings: with two they covered their faces, and with two they covered their feet, and with two they flew. (3) And one called to another and said:
    "Holy, holy, holy is the LORD of hosts;
    the whole earth is full of his glory."

(4)   The pivots on the thresholds shook at the voices of those who called, and the house filled with smoke. (5) And I said: "Woe is me! I am lost, for I am a

man of unclean lips, and I live among a people of
unclean lips; yet my eyes have seen the King, the
LORD of hosts!"

(6)   Then one of the seraphs flew to me, holding a live
coal that had been taken from the altar with a pair
of tongs. (7) The seraph touched my mouth with it
and said, "Now that this has touched your lips, your
guilt has departed and your sin is blotted out."(8)
Then I heard the voice of the Lord saying, "Whom
shall I send, and who will go for us?" And I said,
"Here am I; send me!" (9) And he said, "Go and say
to this people:
        'Keep listening, but do not comprehend;
        keep looking, but do not understand.'

(10) Make the mind of this people dull,
        and stop their ears,
        and shut their eyes,
    so that they may not look with their eyes,
        and listen with their ears,
    and comprehend with their minds,
        and turn and be healed."

(11) Then I said, "How long, O Lord?" And he said:
    "Until cities lie waste without inhabitant,
        and houses without people,
        and the land is utterly desolate;

(12) until the LORD sends everyone far away,
        and vast is the emptiness in the midst of the
        land."

At the very beginning of our study we must confront
the selectivity of lectionary readings: when this chapter appears, the readings usually take only the first eight
verses.[2] These verses make comparatively easy reading,
and in fact have often been used as a model for one's
encounter with God. Verses 9–12, by contrast, make
terribly hard reading, as we can see. But it is important

to try to grasp the whole of Isaiah's experience, so we shall try to take it all in.

The whole passage is full of picturesque details that give us some sense of the thought-world in which Isaiah lived. His inaugural experience took place "in the year that King Uzziah died." Uzziah had ruled for over forty years (783–742 BCE) in Jerusalem over the kingdom of Judah. He was an able and popular ruler, remaining at peace with his counterpart in the northern kingdom of Samaria, King Jeroboam II. Trade flourished, and the land was prosperous past anyone's previous experience. But during the last period of his life Uzziah was afflicted with an incurable skin disease and had to be isolated (2 Kings 15:5); his son Jotham evidently served as co-regent.

Then Uzziah died. One can surmise that Isaiah felt the same kind of shock and disorientation that older Americans will recall having felt when President Kennedy was assassinated in 1963. What will we do, now that Uzziah is gone? What kind of king will Jotham be? With such concerns Isaiah had his vision of the divine king, YAHWEH, in the Temple.

Isaiah says he "saw" the Lord sitting on a throne. Now we should understand that biblical Hebrew lacks a distinction between inner, visionary seeing and the seeing of outer, photographable objects. Both are seen, both are perceived. The Israelites hardly ever seem to have asked whether a given instance of seeing was, as we would say, subjective or objective. Instead, they asked, "Is *God* communicating through this perception?" That was the important thing. We must go on to affirm that many people in this world, in other cultures and in our own, report visionary experiences. Sometimes such experiences are purely personal and casual, but sometimes they trigger a total reorientation of one's life. Such was the case with Isaiah. This was the beginning of his career as a prophet. Nevertheless Isaiah was extraordinarily bold in his description. One hundred and fifty years later, another prophet, Ezekiel, was careful to indicate that what he saw in a similar inaugural vision was a good four steps removed from reality: "This was the appearance of the likeness of the glory of the LORD" (Ezekiel 1:28b). Such indirectness was not for Isaiah: "I saw the Lord!" Interestingly there were Jewish rabbis in later centuries, as we shall see, that were bothered by Isaiah's boldness here, since in Exodus 33:20 God tells Moses, "No one shall see me and live." But Isaiah affirmed his perception straight-out, indeed reinforced it in v. 5.

And he saw the Lord "sitting on a throne," that is, he envisioned God as a king. Today our notion of "king" is not very focused. Kings are for us the stuff of fairy tales, of Shakespeare's plays, of faded photographs of royalty gathering for the funeral of Queen Victoria. It takes an effort of the imagination to remind ourselves that in Isaiah's day the king was the government—the ruler, usually the absolute ruler—and that authority and responsibility rested in him. His job was to command. One of the amazing things about the Servant of God, whom Second Isaiah would later describe (see Chapter 5) is that he shall so astonish kings that they will "shut their mouths" because of him (52:15). Who ever heard of kings shutting their mouths? One of the chief metaphors for God in the Old Testament is naturally "king," inasmuch as God rules the world (Psalm 93:1–2).

Yet more is at stake here than the simple question of God's governance of the world: we need to think about the relationship between the divine king and human kings in those days. Three points must be stressed. The first is

that in the earliest days of Israel the only king they
acknowledged was God. After God revealed his name
(YAHWEH) to Moses, God made a covenant with the people, that is, a treaty or contract. God would support and
protect the Israelites if they obeyed the stipulations of the
treaty. This covenant was modeled on the treaties that
emperors made in those days with vassal states that were
under their control. In this metaphor, Israel was the vassal and owed allegiance to Yahweh specifically. Yahweh
then functioned for Israel as a human king elsewhere
would do for his nation. In Judges 8:22–23 the hero
Gideon refused the offer of kingship because only YAH-
WEH was to be king!

The second point is that things became more complicated when human kingship was inaugurated in Israel
under Saul. Human kingship was seen at least by some
people as an emergency measure when the Philistines,
who had settled on the coast, threatened to swamp the
Israelites (1 Samuel 9:15–26). But if there was to be a
human king at all, he was expected to withstand the
temptation to absolutize his status. He would conform to
the covenant just as every other Israelite did. This was the
message of the prophet Nathan when he accused King
David in the affair with Bathsheba (2 Samuel
11:1–12:23). Thus, when King Uzziah died, it was altogether natural that Isaiah's thoughts would turn from
human to divine kingship.

The third and most crucial point is that if the shift of
kings in Judah caught people's concern, the constant
threat of the king of Assyria caused people to panic.
Assyria was the huge empire in Isaiah's time, centered in
what is today northern Iraq. There was nothing in mem-
ory to match the brutal bullying of nations by the kings
of Assyria. We must postpone a full discussion of Assyria

until Chapter 3, but it is important to say now that the king of Assyria could send people's morale down to zero with a mere glance. If Isaiah's vision was convincing and conclusive, then it follows that the king of Assyria was not really the strongest personage in the universe; YAHWEH was, sitting upon his throne. God was stronger than Assyria. This simple conviction would rule Isaiah's life for forty years and more.

Not only is God king, God is high and lofty, high above everything else. In one extended poem (2:6–22), the central portion of which is included in the Episcopal lectionary,[3] Isaiah describes God rampaging, not only to bring humankind down to size (vv. 11, 17), but indeed to bring down everything that is tall, even high fortified walls (v. 15) and sea-going ships with tall masts (v. 16). Isaiah is so caught up in the notion of immense vertical distance separating God from everything earthly and human that there is simply no comparison. Many people today take it for granted that God is some kind of senior pal. Isaiah would have none of that.

In vv. 2–3 we hear of the seraphs and their hymn to God. We can be sure that Isaiah did not imagine seraphs like angels in a Renaissance painting, but we actually have no idea how he did envision them. One curiosity in the description here is that "feet" is a euphemism for the genitals (compare 7:20, where "hair of the feet" refers to pubic hair). The seraphs cover their faces against the glow given forth by God, they cover their nakedness, and they fly. All we can say for sure is that, like an earthly king, God the heavenly king has courtiers.

Isaiah perceives them to sing, "Holy, holy, holy is the LORD of hosts; the whole earth is full of his glory." This hymn has entered deeply into both Jewish and Christian liturgies. Jewish morning prayer includes it—it is part of the prayer called *Kedushah* ("holiness," since "holy" in Hebrew is *kadosh*). In both the Christian East and West, it is central to the eucharistic liturgy: in the East it is called the *Trisagion* (from the Greek *tris* "three times" and *hagion* "holy"); in the West the *Sanctus* (Latin for "holy"). This hymn has been particularly dear to Christians. There is an extension of this scene in the vision of the glory of God in Revelation 4; indeed in v. 8 of that chapter we hear the four living creatures, each with six wings, sing, day and night, "Holy, holy, holy, the Lord God the Almighty, who was and is and is to come." It is noteworthy that Christians have taken the threefold repetition of "holy" to communicate the Trinity.[4]

It is important to understand that for Isaiah "holy" did not suggest so much the idea of "ethically pure," as it does for us, but rather what is characteristic of God, what is special to God, what is separate from all common or ordinary use. Of course in this measure, God is by definition "holy," but we are not dealing with logic here; rather, we are dealing with the language of religious witness. Isaiah perceived God's courtiers to be affirming God's absolute distinctiveness, God's distance from the ordinariness of the world.

The phrase "the LORD of hosts" is a traditional one in Israel (compare 2 Samuel 6:2), but it is so old that nobody knows what "hosts" refers to.[5] One could guess that the hosts are either other divine beings to whom YAHWEH is superior, or are the armies of Israel which YAHWEH commanded in early "holy" wars, or (at a later stage of Israelite religion) are angels of some sort. Perhaps this traditional designation of God received varying interpretations in the course of Israel's history, but in any event YAHWEH's courtiers used a traditional form of address.

"Glory" (Hebrew *kabod*) is another word whose original range of meaning may be lost on us. In the first place it suggests "weight" or "heaviness." For instance, in 22:24 we read, "And they will hang on him the whole weight (*kabod*) of his ancestral house." Just as we speak of "weighty" people, people of influence and standing, who make a great impression, so the Hebrew word includes the idea of "respect" and "distinction." To give glory to someone is to show him or her respect (compare Proverbs 26:8, where the word is translated "honor"). Since in Isaiah's day those to whom respect was due, such as kings, usually wore rich, splendid robes, contributing to their magnificent appearance, the word takes on the idea of dazzling splendor. Thus in Genesis 31:1 we read, "Jacob has gained all this wealth," and in Isaiah 35:2 we read of the "glory" of Lebanon—her forests of stately cedars make a deep impression. If tall cedars or kings make a great impression, Isaiah affirms that God makes the greatest impression of all. Indeed the whole earth resonates with the impression God makes. God's dazzling splendor is apparent to all with eyes to see. Isaiah saw! The seraphs could see, but hid their eyes. Isaiah's ears rang with their shout.

The picturesque details continue: the pivots on the thresholds shook, and the house filled with smoke (v. 4). We notice the repetition of "fill": "the hem of his robe *filled* the temple" (v. 1), "the whole earth is *full* of his glory" (v. 3), and now the temple is *"filled* with smoke"(v. 4). Everything is filled with manifestations of God.

No wonder Isaiah shrinks in dismay; his reaction is "Woe is me! I am lost!" (v. 5). This verb has two ranges of meaning. One is "I am destroyed" (so Moab in 15:1, where the same verb occurs—the New Revised Standard Version says "I am undone"); the other is "I am struck dumb." This second meaning is appropriate in view of the phrases that follow, which are concerned with Isaiah's lips. Isaiah feels crushed and silent in the face of this experience.

The verse continues, "I am a man of unclean lips, and I live among a people of unclean lips; yet my eyes have seen the King, the LORD of hosts!" Why lips? we wonder. Why not heart, or soul, or ways? This use of "lips" is clearly central to Isaiah, since in vv. 6 and 7 his lips are purified. The first and easiest answer is of course that if he is to speak for God, then his lips must be rendered fit for the task. But the matter runs deeper and goes to the core of the Israelite view of how people function under God.

To the Israelite, what a person thinks up, and then says, and then does, are all part of the same experience. Plans, and words, and actions are all aspects of the same homogenized, personal expression. Plans begin in the heart, which is the seat of the will (and not simply of the emotions). Then plans are put into words. Proverbs 16:23 says it (and here I use the King James Version): "The heart of the wise teacheth his mouth, and addeth learning to his lips." Words have power. In Leviticus 19:14 we learn that cursing a deaf person is just as harmful as putting a stumbling-block out before a blind person. In our culture we speak of idle words, but for the Israelites words have power. People need to say what they mean. Isaiah will later denounce people who say "bitter" when they mean "sweet" (5:20) or perhaps even begin to believe that "bitter" *is* "sweet." Jesus taught that words are crucial. He diverted his hearers' attention from the problem of clean and unclean foods that go into people's mouths to the problem of words that come out of their mouths (Mark 7:14–23). Indeed in Hebrew the very word "word" (*dabar*) also means "thing." Words have power.

So here is Isaiah, struck dumb by a sense of the presence of the high and holy God, a God beside whom all human beings shrink in size, a God whose covenant partner is a people who prove themselves unclean. "Unclean"

here does not mean what we mean by "dirty;" it means
what is ritually unclean, what has no place in God's presence. The poor leper must cover his upper lip and cry out,
"unclean" (Leviticus 13:45). Does Isaiah here hint that
before God the whole people is leprous? Certainly they
all share polluted thoughts, polluted words, polluted acts,
and are unfit to stand before God.

In this situation Isaiah sees himself as no different
from anybody else. So far as this narrative goes, he has
no sense of being special, of being more religious, of
being privileged to gain a glimpse of God. No, he is simply Everyman. Alongside of infinity, every finite number
is the same, whether it be one or a million.

Nevertheless, Isaiah must be rendered fit to speak on
behalf of God, and so the details of his vision continue.
Verses 6–7 tell of his purification. One of the seraphs
touches his mouth with a live coal and pronounces the
words, "Now that this has touched your lips, your guilt
has departed and your sin is blotted out." Isaiah's lips had
been unclean because of "guilt" and "sin." The distance
between God and the people has not been simply a matter of taboos broken but of a profound disorientation
resulting from rebellion, disobedience, and willful ignorance. Isaiah, as a member of Israel, has inevitably taken
part in Israel's sin. But now he is purged and rendered fit
to speak for God, not, we note well, by anything he himself was able to do, but by the action of one of God's
courtiers. It is by grace that he is purified, not by works.

In v. 8, God speaks. It is striking—the divine King has
been present the whole time but has not spoken or acted.
The courtiers have spoken and acted instead. In the climax of Isaiah's vision, God finally speaks, asking for a volunteer to take on the task of messenger. "Whom shall I
send, and who will go for us?" (v. 8). Why, we wonder,

does God say "I" in the first clause and then shift to the plural "us" in the second? Who is this "us," if God alone is exalted in glory? Evidently it is the same "us" as in Genesis 1:26, "Let *us* make humankind in *our* image." Of course this plural, coming after the "holy, holy, holy" in v. 3, has reinforced for Christians the notion that it is the Trinity (just as Christians have traditionally recognized the Trinity in Genesis 1). Evidently Isaiah simply perceived God to speak with a royal "we," on climactic occasions, including his courtiers in these august acts.

"Whom shall I send, and who will go?" God asks. The answer is obvious, since it is Isaiah whose lips have been made fit. To a whimsical reader God's call for a volunteer seems to resemble those occasions I remember in the army when the sergeant calls out, "I want four volunteers—you, you, you, and you." Yet Isaiah could have said "no" to God, as Jeremiah would do on a subsequent occasion (Jeremiah 1:6). Instead, Isaiah steps forward willingly to volunteer: "Here I am, send me!" He is free to accept, even though God has taken the initiative and prepared the way.

Let us pause here to consider what it would have meant for someone to undertake the task of being God's messenger. There were always prophets in Israel. Many early figures were remembered as prophets: Abraham (Genesis 20:7), Moses (Deuteronomy 18:18), Aaron (Exodus 7:1). There were ecstatic bands of prophets in the days of Saul (1 Samuel 10:5). Even more relevant to Isaiah's situation was the precedent of men like Nathan, who spoke out God's word to King David (see especially 2 Samuel 12:1–23), and Elijah, who spoke out God's word to King Ahab in the north (1 Kings 18 and 21). As I have already said, these prophets took it for granted that even though the king is God's anointed, God expects the same standards of behavior to apply to king as to commoner.

Now if, as I have stated, "word" and "thing" are homogenized, then God's words, like God's actions, are supremely powerful. Read 9:8: "The Lord sent a word against Jacob, and it fell on Israel," and read vv. 9–10 to see the damage it caused. In this poem, the "falling" of God's word on Israel is parallel to the "falling" of bricks. Isaiah is called to be a channel for this word-with-power. Isaiah is to be God's mouthpiece for his generation.

What is his message to be? We read it in vv. 9–12, the verses that are usually omitted from the lectionary readings (see note 2). The message is appalling. No wonder these verses are usually left untouched! "Go and say to this people: 'Keep listening, but do not comprehend; keep looking, but do not understand.' Make the mind of this people full, and stop their ears, and shut their eyes, so that they may not look with their eyes, and listen with the ears, and comprehend with the minds, and turn and be healed" (vv. 9–10). It is, in a way, reassuring to learn that the rabbis in ancient times had trouble with this message, too, and softened it in various ways (I shall return to the matter in Chapter 7).

Two matters claim our attention here. The first is that Isaiah is just as appalled as we are. "Then I said, 'How long, O Lord?' And he said, 'Until cities lie waste, without inhabitant.'" (v. 11). What kind of monstrous preaching is this? Is this really Isaiah's call—to preach in such a way that the more he preaches, the less people understand? To push them to destruction? God gives Isaiah a negative assignment: to give people ignorance. What kind of call is this? Alert Christians will recall that vv. 9–10 are used in Mark 4:12 to explain why Jesus spoke in parables, though if one compares this verse in Mark with its parallels in Matthew 13:13 and Luke 8:10, one notices that these two gospels tone down

Mark's rhetoric in different ways (I shall return to Mark's use of these verses in Chapter 8).

The second matter is simply to realize that Isaiah's total view of God is not necessarily one with which we are comfortable. Elsewhere Isaiah affirmed that God's work is strange and alien (28:21, part of a passage we shall examine in Chapter 3). According to a striking passage we shall look at below, Isaiah understood that God was about to trample down the vineyard, which is Israel and Judah and to make it a waste (5:1–7). There are comparable passages elsewhere in the Old Testament. In Exodus 10:1, God "hardens" Pharaoh's heart, and the word "harden" there is the one that is translated "stop" their ears here in Isaiah 6:10. Though it is difficult, we might stretch our view of God to compass the idea that God intended Pharaoh to be wicked, since Pharaoh was Israel's enemy. But how can we accept the idea that God intends Israel, the covenant people, to be ignorant? We are tempted to believe that Isaiah misunderstood God!

Here is a way to get at the problem: Isaiah is commanded, it seems, to be an *anti*-prophet, to do the opposite of what a prophet ordinarily does. The people who turned out to be all that God's people should not be, an *anti*-people, deserve an anti-prophet.[6]

Of course such a grim program contrasts with to Isaiah's actual positive effect. The prophet's words were preserved, after all, preserved to be available to us. In the long run he was not only an anti-prophet. The fact that he gave one of his sons the symbolic name Shear-jashub (7:3), which means "a remnant shall turn," contradicts the word here in 6:10 that the people are not to "turn and be healed." Later, when this son was born, Isaiah must have heard a mitigation of the terrible command. The point is this: at the time of his call, Isaiah really perceived that

God's patience was at an end and that anything hastening
the day of judgment was good—such was the purpose of
Isaiah's ministry.

GOD'S PEOPLE ISRAEL HAVE BROKEN THE
NORMS OF THE COVENANT

We are not yet at a point to decide whether Isaiah misunderstood God or not. We must expand the beachhead
of passages in which he details the breakdown of community within the covenant people. Such passages are
found throughout chapters 1–39, notably in chapters 1,
3, 5, 9–10, and 28–31. These passages center principally
on matters of social justice and the irresponsibility of the
people's leaders. Curiously, very few of these passages are
found in our lectionaries. The selection we hear does not
give Isaiah's social message a full hearing.

Look at 10:1–4. The first word, "Ah," really means
"Woe":

(1) Ah, you who make iniquitous decrees,
          who write oppressive statutes,

(2) to turn aside the needy from justice
          and to rob the poor of my people of their right,
     that widows may be your spoil,
          and that you may make the orphans your prey!

(3) What will you do on the day of punishment,
          in the calamity that will come from far away?
     To whom will you flee for help,
          and where will you leave your wealth,

(4) so as not to crouch among the prisoners
          or fall among the slain?
     For all this his anger has not turned away;
          his hand is stretched out still.

This passage, and others, like 5:8–10, are stunning indictments of a society in which the rich have grown richer and the poor poorer, but 5:8–10 and 10:1–4 are not included in any lectionary reading. Nor is the opening passage of the whole book, 1:2–4, included. The words still sting; when it comes to loyalty to God's will, Israel is dumber than the dumb ox (1:3)!

Let us take two passages that *are* included in lectionary readings. I suggest that these will help us understand the terrible call Isaiah heard. The first is 1:10–20. At least portions of this passage are found in some lectionaries.[7] Let us concentrate first on vv. 10–17:

(10) Hear the word of the LORD,
      you rulers of Sodom!
   Listen to the teaching of our God,
      you people of Gomorrah!

(11) What to me is the multitude of your sacrifices?
      says the LORD;
   I have had enough of burnt offerings of rams
      and the fat of fed beasts;
   I do not delight in the blood of bulls,
      or of lambs, or of goats.

(12) When you come to appear before me,
      who asked this from your hand?
   Trample my courts no more;

(13) bringing offerings is futile;
      incense is an abomination to me.
   New moon and sabbath and calling of
   convocation—
      I cannot endure solemn assemblies
      with iniquity.

(14) Your new moons and your appointed festivals
      my soul hates;
   they have become a burden to me,
      I am weary of bearing them.

(15) When you stretch out your hands,
> I will hide my eyes from you;
> even though you make many prayers,
> > I will not listen;
> your hands are full of blood.

(16) Wash yourselves; make yourselves clean;
> > remove the evil of your doings
> > from before my eyes;
> cease to do evil,

(17)   ·learn to do good;
> seek justice,
> > rescue the oppressed,
> defend the orphan,
> > plead for the widow.

Isaiah begins by addressing his people as Sodom and Gomorrah—cities blasted by God for their wickedness in the distant past. What would a modern equivalent be— brother and sister Huns, perhaps? Then the prophet moves in to criticize the people for their religious rituals— their sacrifices, their festivals (which God says his soul hates), and even their prayers (v. 15). In those days, the "stretching out" of hands was the attitude of prayer. God hates those hands which are bloody with social injustice. In short, Isaiah, in the name of God, rebukes the people for being religious, as that trait is ordinarily understood. In a stunning series of short lines of only two Hebrew words each, a simplified check-list for the dullard, he ticks off God's rules (vv. 16–17). What would these two-word phrases be in English? "Stop evil! Learn good! Seek justice! Rescue victims! Defend orphans! Help widows!"

To this scathing denunciation is appended vv. 18–20:

(18) Come now, let us argue it out,
> says the LORD:

> though your sins are like scarlet,
>> they shall be like snow;
> though they are red like crimson,
>> they shall become like wool.
>
> (19) If you are willing and obedient,
>> you shall eat the good of the land;
>
> (20) but if you refuse and rebel,
>> you shall be devoured by the sword;
>> for the mouth of the Lord has spoken.

Verse 18 is normally taken to offer mitigating hope, especially after vv. 10–17. But the implication for Isaiah's hearers may have been less hopeful. "Let us argue it out" implies a legal case between God and the people. The twice-occurring "though" in v. 18 is a simple "if" in Hebrew, and the tone of these lines suggests that the judge is quoting the people's own argument: "If your sins are like scarlet, they shall be like snow—is *this* your line of thinking?" In vv. 19–20 come the big ifs: "*If* you are willing and obedient, you shall eat the good of the land; but *if* you refuse and rebel, you shall be devoured [literally "eaten"] by the sword." If these three verses were heard in the same mood as vv. 10–17, then the big if of v. 19, "*if* you are willing and obedient," hardly holds out a realistic hope.

Before we decide that Isaiah is a tiresome scold, we need to look at one more passage in detail, 5:1–7. It is included in all the lectionaries.[8] This is, perhaps, the best presentation of Isaiah's perception of the breakdown of community in Israel and Judah.

> (1) Let me sing for my beloved
>> my love-song concerning his vineyard:
> My beloved had a vineyard
>> on a very fertile hill.

(2) He dug it and cleared it of stones,
         and planted it with choice vines;
     he built a watchtower in the midst of it,
         and hewed out a wine vat in it;
     he expected it to yield grapes,
         but it yielded wild grapes.

(3) And now, inhabitants of Jerusalem
         and people of Judah,
     judge between me
         and my vineyard.

(4) What more was there to do for my vineyard
         that I have not done in it?
     When I expected it to yield grapes,
         why did it yield wild grapes?

(5) And now I will tell you
         what I will do to my vineyard.
     I will remove its hedge,
         and it shall be devoured;
     I will break down its wall,
         and it shall be trampled down.

(6) I will make it a waste;
         it shall not be pruned or hoed,
         and it shall be overgrown with briers and thorns;
     I will also command the clouds
         that they rain no rain upon it.

(7) For the vineyard of the Lord of hosts
         is the house of Israel,
     and the people of Judah
         are his pleasant planting;
     he expected justice,
         but saw bloodshed;
     righteousness,
         but heard a cry!

Isaiah takes the part of someone singing to his beloved
(the Hebrew word is masculine) a love-song concerning

his vineyard (v. 1). Who is the beloved, and what is this all about? On the face of it, Isaiah could be singing a song about a friend in the context of the harvest festival, the feast of ingathering (Exodus 23:16b, also called the festival of booths). Or, it might be a wedding-song concerning the bridegroom. Evidently the image of vineyard often referred to the bride (compare Song of Solomon 8:11–12). Or, again, Isaiah may be embarked on a parody of a fertility-cult hymn, in which case the beloved would presumably be the fertility god Baal. But, as we see in the last verse of the song, it turns out to have a stinger. If Isaiah is talking about a friend at harvest time, then the friend will turn out to be God. If Isaiah is talking about a bridegroom, then the bridegroom will turn out to be God. If Isaiah is talking in pagan terms about a fertility deity, then the real deity who gives fertility will turn out to be the true God. In any event, the first verse offers attractive, lush vocabulary.

On the surface verse 2 is a description of the patient work of a vineyard keeper digging, terracing, planting, building a tower to guard against thieves and birds. He planted "choice vines" to bear lush red grapes. Given the fact that the vineyard keeper will turn out to be God (which we know by looking ahead to v. 7), we can ponder here the patient work of God in settling the people in the promised land, steadily caring for them, and persevering with them through the years. In particular, in the phrase "he expected it to yield grapes," "expected" is not strong enough. The Hebrew verb means "long for." God *longs* for the vine to turn out right; but it doesn't—it yields literally "rotten stinkers!"

Verses 3–4 involve the hearers in the problem: What should I do, you farmers, that I have neglected to do? Now comes the first hint that there is more requested here than mere agricultural advice. The hearers are asked to judge between the vineyard keeper and his vineyard, as if there is a dispute between them. The same phrase is used in Genesis 16:5 in a squabble between Abraham and Sarah. Why did the grapes want to go and turn bad? The phrases of v. 2 are repeated for emphasis: God *longs* for the vine to turn out right, when it doesn't.

Verses 5–6 return to the agricultural work of v. 2, but whereas before it was constructive work, now it is destructive. The vineyard keeper will remove the hedge, break down the wall, and stop the pruning and hoeing, so that the vineyard becomes a waste. Furthermore, in a second, much more awful hint that agriculture is not the sole concern, the vineyard keeper will command the rain to stop. Farmers hope for rain, wait for rain, pray for rain—what kind of farmer is this who will turn off the rain, who *can* turn off the rain? The fertility deity was supposed to turn on the rain, but since God is the real God who controls the rain, it is God who can and will turn off the rain.

This is not a human vineyard keeper at all, of course (v. 7), and his true identity now tumbles out in a single line, "The vineyard of the LORD of hosts is the house of Israel." Given the key, we can deal with all the earlier details of the song in the way we are intended to. In seven Hebrew words (v. 7b) we have the climax: the good grapes that God longed for (vv. 2, 4) are really justice and righteousness. That is what God really longs for, but what he got was rotten grapes, the opposite of justice and righteousness—bloodshed and the cry of the oppressed. This climactic final half-verse, we need to know, carries a double pun in Hebrew. He expected *mishpat*, but instead got *mispah*; he expected *zedaqa* but instead got *ze'aqa*. Two British scholars have tried their hand at putting the puns into English: Ronald Knox, a Roman Catholic translator, offered this: "He looked to find right reason there, and all was treason; to find plain dealing, and he heard only the plaint of the oppressed"; George Box, a biblical commentator, did even better: "For measures He looked—but lo massacres! For right—but lo riot."[9]

One more point needs to be made about this passage. We have noted the occurrences of the verb I translated "long for" in vv. 2, 4, and 7. What I have not yet said is that these three occurrences of the verb are the only ones in the whole Old Testament that have God for the subject. All the other occurrences use it for the longing of human beings. Many people of faith today have trouble imagining how God's loving care for his people can be squared with his wrathful anger at his people. Isaiah had no such problem. The God of grace, who expends all that labor to clear the hillside of stones to plant and tend the vineyard, longing for lush red grapes, is all the while the same God of judgment who, if the grapes turn out bad, has no choice but to pull down the stone walls and allow the briers and thorns to choke the vineyard. God cares, God longs, God waits. But the covenant people disappoint. The grapes are worthless, rotten fruit. What else is there to do?

As we listen to this song, questions crowd our minds. What would have been the reaction of the first hearers of the song, people who, Isaiah was convinced, were people of unclean lips? How many of them would have decided he was a *false* prophet, someone who misunderstood God? We wonder. The question in our minds, the question that surfaced when we heard that terrible call to obfuscate people, the question of whether he might have misunderstood God might have surfaced in the minds of his first hearers, too. But the text of his call has survived; it stands! Given the three ways to hear Old Testament texts that I set forth in Chapter 1, can we say that now we *really* understand what the text of Isaiah's call means?

We must save struggling with these questions till we have a fuller grasp of Isaiah's message. Earlier I mentioned that behind Isaiah's call narrative loomed the king of Assyria. We must come to terms with Assyria. We must also take account of the kind of hope that Isaiah finally foresaw for his people. It is to these topics that we turn in Chapter 3.

NOTES

1. See recently Brevard S. Childs, *Isaiah* (Old Testament Library; Louisville, KY: Westminster John Knox, 2001), 260–66.

2. Verses 1–8 are appointed for Trinity Sunday in Year B in the Revised Common Lectionary, and in Year C in the Episcopalian Lectionary. Iit is not a reading for Trinity Sunday for Roman Catholics. It is also the reading for the Sunday between February 4 and 10 in Year C in the Revised Common Lectionary and the Rpoman Catholic lectionary, but it is to be noted that on that Sunday the Revised Common Lectionary recommends reading the whole chapter, vv. 9–13 and well as vv. 1–8. Verses 1–8 are also reading the Roman Catholic weekday lectionary on the Saturday between July 9 and 15 in Year II.

3. Isaiah 2:10–17, Episcopal Lectionary, Year A, Sunday between June 26 and July 2.

4. Hence its use on Trinity Sunday; see note 2.

5. See the discussion in Helmer Ringgren, *Israelite Religion* (Philadelphia: Fortress, 1966), 68–69.

6. This is the suggestion of Edwin M. Good, *Irony in the Old Testament* (London: S.P.C.K., 1965; 2nd ed., Sheffield: The Almond Press, 1981), 136–137.

7. All eleven verses are found in the Revised Common Lectionary for the Sunday within August 7 to 13 in Year C, and in the Episcopal Lectionary for the Sunday within October 29 to November 5 in Year C. In the daily lectionary of Roman Catholics vv. 10 and 16–20

are heard on Tuesday in the Second Week in Lent, and vv. 10–17 are heard on the Monday within July 11–17 in Year II.

8. It is found in the Revised Common Lectionary for the Sunday between August 14 and 20 in Year C, associated with Jesus' words on the end of the age, Luke 12:49–56, "I came to bring fire to the earth"; and in the Roman Catholic, Episcopal, and Lutheran lectionaries for the Sunday between October 2 and 8 in Year A, associated with Jesus' parable of the vineyard, Matthew 21:33–43.

9. Ronald Knox (translator), *The Holy Bible* (New York: Sheed & Ward, 1956); George H. Box, *The Book of Isaiah* (London: Isaac Pitman & Sons, 1908) 41.

Chapter 3

Assyria Is on the March—Is There Any Hope?

IN CHAPTER 2 WE TOOK NOTE of the hesitation of the lectionaries to include the last part of Isaiah 6 and to include Isaiah's words on social injustice. There is an even more remarkable silence in the lectionaries, and that is in their silence on Assyria. In Isaiah 1–39 there are forty-three occurrences of the words "Assyria," "Assyrian," and "Assyrians." Nineteen of these, it is true, are in the historical chapters 36–39, chapters that are largely taken from 2 Kings and that would therefore not be used in the lectionary. This still leaves twenty-four occurrences within chapters 1–35.

These occurrences are passed by, with one bare exception, a complicated exception that is worth our consideration. It involves the Old Testament reading for the fourth Sunday of Advent. In all the lectionaries, the Old

Testament reading for that Sunday is the passage in Isaiah 7 that contains the prophet's word to King Ahaz about the child to be born who will be called Immanuel. The core of that passage, namely v. 14, is taken by the Gospel of Matthew to be a reference to the virgin birth (Matthew 1:22–23), and indeed in all the lectionaries the Gospel reading for that Sunday is Matthew 1:18–25.[1]

As we shall see in a moment, the immediate circumstance for Isaiah was rather different than the one perceived by Matthew. The last verse of the Isaiah passage, 7:17, set the stage. This verse reads, "The LORD will bring on you and on your ancestral house such days as have not come since the day that Ephraim departed from Judah—the king of Assyria."[2] That mention of Assyria in Isaiah 1:17 is the only one to survive the Christian winnowing of the lectionaries. Given the occasion on which Christians hear Isaiah 7:10–17, namely the last Sunday before Christmas, it is hard to imagine that this one bare mention of the king of Assyria would inspire the terror that it did when the passage was drafted in Old Testament times. Our first task, then, is to resurrect that terror.

GOD IS BRINGING ASSYRIA UPON THE NATION AS A PUNISHMENT

Assyria was one of the two superpowers in the region—the other was Egypt—and Isaiah lived at a time when Assyria's power was expanding to its utmost. From her center in what is today northern Iraq, her realm had spread south to the Persian Gulf, northeast to touch Lake Urmia in present-day Iran, north to Lake Van in what is now eastern Turkey, and west toward the Mediterranean Sea. Even beyond these frontiers she exacted tribute from vassals and client tribes and nations, such as the Medes in central Iran.

We are concerned here with the western expansion of Assyria toward Judah. One reason for her expansion was, of course, sheer expansionism. A dynamic empire constantly wants more (as Hitler's did before and during World War II), but there were specific reasons for Assyria's wish to gain a foothold on the Mediterranean. The mountains of Lebanon held timber wealth. Access to sea trade on the Mediterranean would lower transport costs. And troops could be stationed to prevent any possible northward expansion by Egypt. Palestine was always the no-man's-land between Egypt and the superpower in the east, just as Poland has been between Germany and Russia.

In the century before Isaiah, Assyria marched west to loot and punish, but in Isaiah's lifetime Assyria marched west for permanent conquest. The first crisis came roughly eight years after Isaiah's call, in 734/733 BCE. The crisis, in fact, lies behind Isaiah 7:1–17. Because the passage is crucial for Christians, it is important to read the whole sequence in order to grasp the historical situation out of which it comes to us.[3]

> (1)   In the days of Ahaz son of Jotham son of Uzziah, king of Judah, King Rezin of Aram and King Pekah son of Remaliah of Israel went up to attack Jerusalem, but could not mount an attack against it. (2) When the house of David heard that Aram had allied itself with Ephraim, the heart of Ahaz and the heart of his people shook as the trees of the forest shake before the wind.

> (3)   The LORD said to Isaiah, Go out to meet Ahaz, you and your son Shear-jashub, at the end of the conduit of the upper pool on the highway to the Fuller's Field, (4) and say to him, Take heed, be quiet, do not fear, and do not let your heart be faint because of these two smoldering stumps of firebrands, because of the fierce anger of Rezin and Aram and the son of Remaliah. (5) Because Aram— with Ephraim and the son of Remaliah—has plotted

evil against you, saying, (6) Let us go up against
Judah and cut off Jerusalem and conquer it for
ourselves and make the son of Tabeel king in it; (7)
therefore thus says the Lord GOD:
> It shall not stand,
> and it shall not come to pass.

(8) For the head of Aram is Damascus,
> and the head of Damascus is Rezin.
(Within sixty-five years Ephraim will be shattered,
no longer a people.)

(9) The head of Ephraim is Samaria,
> and the head of Samaria is the son of Remaliah.
If you do not stand firm in faith,
> You shall not stand at all.

(10) Again the Lord spoke to Ahaz, saying, (11) Ask a
sign of the Lord your God; let it be deep as Sheol
or high as heaven. (12) But Ahaz said, I will not
ask, and I will not put the Lord to the test. (13)
Then Isaiah said: "Hear then, O house of David! Is
it too little for you to weary mortals, that you weary
my God also? (14) Therefore the Lord himself will
give you a sign. Look, the young woman is with
child and shall bear a son, and shall name him
Immanuel. (15) He shall eat curds and honey by
the time he knows how to refuse the evil and
choose the good. (16) For before the child knows
how to refuse the evil and choose the good, the
land before whose two kings you are in dread will
be deserted. (17) The Lord will bring on you and
on your people and on your ancestral house such
days as have not come since the day that Ephraim
departed from Judah—the king of Assyria."

Let us not be daunted by those first heavy verses! The
actual facts are straightforward. Ahaz was the grandson of
the popular King Uzziah (see Chapter 2). He came to the
throne a year or two before this crisis, when he was only

twenty years old. Two older and stronger kings to the north, King Pekah of Israel (whose capital was Samaria) and King Rezin of Syria (whose capital was Damascus), wanted to form an anti-Assyrian coalition. They were convinced that the small kingdoms to the west must hang together against Assyria, or they would all hang separately, so they pressured King Ahaz in Jerusalem to join their coalition. To this end they invaded Judah and besieged Jerusalem, though without success. Ahaz was nevertheless shaking in his boots (vv. 1–2, 6).

Isaiah responded to God's call to meet Ahaz and reassure him that these two kings in the north were (as the Chinese expression has it) "paper tigers," not worth worrying over. In effect, his message was that the two nations in question were nothing more than their capital cities, and the cities were nothing more than their kings, and the kings were not nine feet tall (vv. 3–8). He closed the message by giving the king a little Hebrew saying about standing firm in faith (v. 9).

As we have noted, most of the lectionary readings begin with v. 10. In vv. 11–12 we hear that Ahaz did not "stand firm," refusing even a reassuring sign. The sign was offered anyway, and, because the wording of the sign (v. 14) is so crucial for our understanding, we must take extra care with it. Our translation really does render the Hebrew: "Look, the young woman is with child [that is, is pregnant] and shall bear a son, and shall name him Immanuel."

As we read this verse from Matthew's vantage-point, we need to make three matters clear. First, the translation "young woman" is correct, not the "virgin," as Matthew has it. The Hebrew word in the Isaiah passage refers to a woman of marriageable age, not to a virgin. But the *Greek* translation of the Old Testament, the Septuagint, a translation made about five hundred years after

Isaiah's time (I shall discuss it in Chapter 7), did use "virgin," and Matthew knew his Old Testament in Greek. Second, the young woman is not identified. Isaiah, in speaking to Ahaz, must simply have gestured in her direction. The identity of the woman was clear to the participants, even though that identity is lost for us. And third, Matthew takes the symbolic name Immanuel as a word of good news, as indeed it can be. In Hebrew the word means "God [is] with us" (see Matthew 1:23). Most scholars suspect that behind the good news that we see so easily there lies a complicated history of understanding that we can discern only in part.

The passage has generated all kinds of analysis,[4] and it is doubtful we shall ever achieve absolute certainty concerning the nature of the original event. Let us ponder some probabilities. In recent years there have been fresh suggestions about the passage that appear altogether plausible. The Hebrew word here translated "young woman" is not common. In Ugaritic (a predecessor of Hebrew) it seems to mean "a woman of different ethnicity, alien woman." In Song of Solomon 6:8, three sorts of women in the harem are listed: "sixty queens and eighty concubines, and *maidens* without number" ("maidens" is our word). The suggestion has been made that this last category consists of women brought into the harem by diplomatic exchange.

By this understanding the young woman in Isaiah 7:14 would be such a consort of Ahaz, present by diplomatic exchange, and that she is pregnant by the king. This foreign woman would bear a son with the symbolic name "God is with us," meaning "God is with me [the woman] and my son *rather than* with you [Ahaz]." By this understanding the name would be a word of judgment against Ahaz, who lacked trust in Yahweh (vv. 12–13). It would

suggest that the next king in the line of David who carried Yahweh's legitimacy would not be born from Abi, the
legitimate queen of Ahaz (2 Kings 18:2) but from this foreign woman.

As it turned out, Isaiah had a largely positive experience with the legitimate son of Ahaz, Hezekiah, so, ultimately, the name "Immanuel" was attached to a savior
figure expected in the future.[5] Indeed the careful reader
may discern that vv. 15–17 offer early interpretations of
the sign in v. 14. Verses 15–16 are good news, "By the
time the child is weaned, the threat from the two kings
in the north will be gone." The predictions of "such days"
in the first part of v. 17 could be either good news or bad
news; the last words of v. 17, "the king of Assyria," are
thoroughly bad news. Furthermore, it should be noted
that vv. 18–25 offer four *more* threats amplifying the words
with which v. 17 ends.

This reconstruction of the situations that gave rise to
Isaiah 7 seems needlessly complicated, and Christians
will wonder "what does all this have to do with what we
hear on the Sunday before Christmas?" My answer is that
it is an opportunity to exercise the third way of hearing
Scripture that I offered in Chapter 1. That is, we can discern the intentionality of God in more than one way of
understanding the text. Matthew has taken v. 14 out of
an altogether different context and in a different language, and has used it as a building block in his own theological affirmation. We can honor Matthew even while
we work at reconstructing Isaiah's intention in his original pronouncement.

Let us return now to Ahaz and the events of his days.
Unable to trust Yahweh and heed Isaiah's word, he
begged help from Assyria against King Pekah and King
Rezin. So what happened? Assyria captured Pekah's

Israelite lands in Galilee and Transjordan, probably in
733 BCE, marched against Damascus, Rezin's capital, in
732 and conquered it, and then eleven years later in 721,
marched on Samaria, Pekah's capital, and conquered it.
Isaiah witnessed end of the northern kingdom of Israel,
and Ahaz sent an enormous gift to the king of Assyria,
becoming his vassal (2 Kings 16:7–8).

Now let us carry the story ahead another twenty
years. Ahaz's successor Hezekiah tried to back out of
the vassal relationship with Assyria and to seek help
from Egypt, but in 701 Assyria marched against
Jerusalem. The Assyrian king at that time, Sennacherib,
boasted that he had captured forty-six fortified cities
in Judah and shut King Hezekiah and the remnant of
his troops in Jerusalem "like a bird in a cage."[6] The narrative in 2 Kings 18:13–37 is worth reading in its
entirety to gain some notion of how terrorized Jerusalem was by Assyria.

Strikingly, though, Isaiah did not view Assyria as the
incarnation of evil: rather, he was convinced that her
onslaughts on the territories of Israel and Judah were
God's punishment for their breaking of covenant. In
Chapter 2 we looked at Isaiah 10:1–4. Verse 3 of that
passage has Assyria in mind: "What will you do on the
day of punishment, in the calamity that will come from
far away?" Indeed let us look now at the passage that
directly follows those verses:[7]

> (5)   Ah, Assyria, the rod of my anger—
>   the club in their hands is my fury!
>
> (6)   Against a godless nation I send him,
>   and against the people of my wrath I command
>   him,
>   to take spoil and seize plunder,

and to tread them down like the mire of the
streets.

(7)   But this is not what he intends,
      nor does he have this in mind;
      but it is in his heart to destroy,
      and to cut off nations not a few.

From Isaiah's perspective Assyria was not simply acting
out of the dynamics of conquest. No, Isaiah understands
God to be addressing Assyria as the rod of his anger
against "a godless nation," that is, Israel and Judah!
Assyria was God's instrument of punishment, but Assyria
does not *know* it is God's instrument of punishment.
Assyria's heart is bent simply on destruction. However,

(12) When the Lord has finished all his work on Mount
     Zion and on Jerusalem, he will punish the arrogant
     boasting of the king of Assyria and his haughty
     pride. (13) For he says:
        "By the strength of my hand I have done it,
           and by my wisdom, for I have
           understanding;
        I have removed the boundaries of peoples,
           and have plundered their treasures;
        like a bull I have brought down
           those who sat on thrones.

(14) My hand has found, like a nest,
        the wealth of the peoples;
     and as one gathers eggs that have been forsaken,
        so I have gather all the earth;
     and there was none that moved a wing,
        or opened its mouth, or chirped."

Isaiah declares Assyria to be God's instrument of punishment, but (and this is an enormous "but") when God is
finished using Assyria to punish, it will be Assyria's turn

to receive punishment for its arrogant boasting (v. 12).
Assyria certainly does boast (vv. 13–14)! All this is a subtle theological perspective on international relations.

HOPE FOR ISRAEL'S FUTURE: A PURIFIED JERUSALEM AND A PURIFIED KINGSHIP

Now, given all the bad news that Isaiah communicated,
was there any possibility, in his mind, of *good* news?
What was to be the ultimate fate of the people? In terms
of Isaiah's call, discussed in Chapter 2, was their fate to
be "until cities lie waste without inhabitant" (6:11), or
might the people have the right to hope that at least "a
remnant will return" (the meaning of the name of Isaiah's son mentioned in 7:3)? Evidently the answer is that
there *was* hope, but that it was modest hope on the other
side of the bad news we have surveyed. The problem is
that locating Isaiah's own expressions of hope is difficult,
because later generations evidently seized on Isaiah's
modest hope and built on it their own immoderate visions
of the future, leaving us puzzled as to where Isaiah's own
words leave off and those of others begin.

After all, even the word "remnant" offers an ambigu-
ous impact. It may be good news that, say, ten percent
will survive, but then one ponders the bad news of the
ninety percent who won't. In Chapter 2 we looked at
1:2–4. Israel is dumber than the dumb ox. Verses 5–8 of
that passage continue with a description of terrible military destruction. Then v. 9: "If the LORD of hosts had not
left us a few survivors, we would have been like Sodom,
and become like Gomorrah." Without a few survivors, we
would be dead as a doornail!

Beyond his hope for the survival of a remnant, Isaiah evidently anticipated both a transformed Jerusalem

and a transformed Davidic kingship. Before we turn to passages pointing to these transformations, we must touch on 22:15–23, most of which appears in the Roman Catholic lectionary.[8] In this passage Isaiah states that God will replace a senior nobleman, Shebna (the "master of the household"), with a man named Eliakim, though we can no longer determine the specific circumstances. Let us notice v. 22: "I will place on his [Eliakim's] shoulder the key of the house of David; he shall open, and no one shall shut; he shall shut, and no one shall open." That is to say, he will have exclusive power to open and close the palace and thus control the government offices set up there. The phrasing of this verse shaped the wording of Matthew 16:19, in which Matthew reports Jesus' giving to Peter (his deputy) the "keys of the kingdom of heaven," with the power to "bind" and "loose." The Matthew passage is paired with this Isaiah passage in the lectionary. One may also note that Revelation 3:7 cites the same Isaiah verse. There the reference is to God's giving Jesus "the key of David, who opens and no one will shut, who shuts and no one will open." These are splendid examples of the way New Testament writers have drawn on the words of Isaiah.

Isaiah looked forward to a transformed Jerusalem, hope embedded in the midst of judgment. In Isaiah 1:21 we hear, "How the faithful city has become a whore!" but in v. 26 we hear that "Afterward you shall be called the city of righteousness, the faithful city." These verses in chapter 1 do not survive in any of our lectionary readings.

There is, however, a lectionary reading that does communicate a transformed Jerusalem. It is 28:14–22, a selection in the Episcopal lectionary,[9] again hope embedded in the midst of judgment. Let us look at the first four verses:

(14) Therefore hear the word of the Lord, you scoffers
who rule this people in Jerusalem.

(15) Because you have said, "We have made a covenant
with death,
and with Sheol we have an agreement;
when the overwhelming scourge passes through
it will not come to us;
for we have made lies our refuge,
and in falsehood we have taken shelter";

(16) therefore thus says the Lord GOD,
See, I am laying in Zion a foundation stone,
a tested stone,
a precious cornerstone, a sure foundation:
"One who trusts will not panic."

(17) And I will make justice the line,
and righteousness the plummet;
hail will sweep away the refuge of lies,
and waters will overwhelm the shelter.

Verse 14 offers a remarkable double play on words in
Hebrew. The leaders are addressed as "scoffers," literally
"men of scoffing." Those who heard this would think
immediately of Proverbs. 29:8, where it is said that
"scoffers [again, 'men of scoffing'] set a city aflame." By
implication, these are not rulers but *mis*-rulers. But there
is another twist here, because if the addressees "rule this
people in Jerusalem," one might have expected (by parallelism) that they would be addressed as "men of Zion"
(the central mount of Jerusalem) instead of "men of
scoffing" ("Zion" in Hebrew is *siyyon*, and "scoffing" is
lason). But there is still more. "Those who rule" can also
be heard as "those who make clever sayings." In short, by
twisting "Zion" into "scoffing" and by leaving the possibility
that "rule" is really "make smart cracks," Isaiah makes hash
of the political leadership. (We recall from Chapter 2 that

in 1:10 the leaders were addressed in similar fashion as "rulers of Sodom.")

In v. 15 the passage mocks the implications of a royal proclamation: "We have signed a mutual aid pact with—" with whom? With *Misrayim* (Egypt)? With *Asshur* (Assyria)? "No!" says Isaiah; rather, with *mawet* (death) and with *Sheol* (the grave)—that's all your diplomatic negotiations come to. (We wonder what the particular political circumstances were when Isaiah delivered *this* message.) And where have we found our refuge? In God, who is our refuge and strength (Psalm 46:1)? No, says Isaiah; rather, "We have made lies and falsehood our shelter." So God will sweep away this flimsy, poorly built structure with hail and waters (v. 17b). In its place God is erecting on Zion a shelter with a firm foundation stone (vv. 16–17a). The symbolic name of this stone proclaims salvation for those who trust God. It is the only possible beginning for a transformed Jerusalem.

We should take note here that this word about the special "stone" is picked up in 1 Peter 2:6, where it refers to Jesus Christ. It is important to notice that the next verse in 1 Peter goes on to cite two other references to special "stones" in the Old Testament that the New Testament identifies with Jesus Christ, the "stone that the builders rejected" (Psalm 118:22) and the "stone that makes them stumble" (Isaiah 8:14), and further that Romans 9:33 blends such passages.

We recall Sennacherib's boast that he had taken forty-six walled cities in Judah and shut King Hezekiah up like a bird in a cage. Yet even though Jerusalem was besieged, Isaiah's proclamation of a transformed Jerusalem implied that the city would not fall to the Assyrian army, and so it proved to be. Tradition recalls that the Assyrian army fell victim to a plague (implied by 2 Kings 19:35), though historians argue over the precise details. In any event the deliverance reinforced in Judah the conviction that the city was inviolable (a conviction that would give Jeremiah difficulty a hundred years later when he proclaimed the coming fall of the city (for example, Jeremiah 9:10–11).

Alert readers will think of another passage that depicts a transformed Jerusalem (2:1–5), but most scholars judge this passage to be a later addition to the collection of Isaiah's words, so we shall save it till the beginning of Chapter 4.

Parallel with Isaiah's hope for a transformed Jerusalem is his hope for a transformed Davidic kingship. Indeed this is the hope for which Isaiah is most fondly remembered by Christians. We have already seen how Christians have seized on 7:14 for the gospel. After that verse, the passage in Isaiah that is most fondly remembered by Christians is 9:2–7, "to us a child is born." Given the reminiscences of its phrase in Luke 1:32–33, it is the Old Testament lesson for Christmas Eve or for the first service on Christmas Day in all the lectionaries (though the Episcopal lectionary omits v. 5).[10] This is the passage that I discussed in Chapter 1 as an illustration of the tension between original context and Christian use. It is a passage so associated in the mind of Christians with the birth of Jesus that the exercise hearing of it in Isaiah's original context is exceedingly difficult—and this difficulty is compounded by the fact that we are not able to be as precise as we wish about what that context actually was.

Rather than starting with v. 2, we need the background of v. 1:

> But there will be no gloom for those who were in anguish. In the former time he brought into contempt the land of Zebulun and the land of Naphtali, but in the latter time he will make glorious the way of the sea, the land beyond the Jordan, Galilee of the nations.

Earlier in this chapter I stated that Assyria had captured the Israelite lands in Galilee and Transjordan, probably in 733; these included "the land of Zebulun and the land of Naphtali." But, says this verse, the people who had been demoralized by these losses will have hope again.

Now vv. 2–7. I have already noted the omission of v. 5 in the Episcopal lectionary, and it is important to note that the text of Handel's *Messiah* omits all of vv. 3–5, thus jumping from v. 2 to vv. 6–7. As a result, even when the whole passage is used, the verses that *Messiah* omits tend not to make an impression on us. When we examine all the verses, we realize that it is surprisingly militaristic:

(2)   The people who walked in darkness
            have seen a great light;
        those who lived in a land of deep darkness—
            on them light has shined.

(3)   You have multiplied the nation,
            you have increased its joy;
        they rejoice before you
            as with joy at the harvest,
            as people exult when dividing plunder.

(4)   For the yoke of their burden,
            and the bar across their shoulders,
            the rod of their oppressor,
        you have broken as on the day of Midian.

(5)   For all the boots of the tramping warriors
            and all the garments rolled in blood
        shall be burned as fuel for the fire.

(6)   For a child has been born for us,
            a son given to us;
        authority rests upon his shoulders;
            and he is named
        Wonderful Counselor, Mighty God,
            Everlasting Father, Prince of Peace.

(7)   His authority shall grow continually,
          and there shall be endless peace
      for the throne of David and his kingdom.
      He will establish and uphold it
      with justice and with righteousness
          from this time onward and forevermore.
      The zeal of the LORD of hosts will do this.

God will give the people as much joy as they experience when they plunder after a victory (v. 3). We must
remember that one of the goals of war in ancient times
was plunder. God will renew the nation as it was renewed
long ago when Gideon defeat the Midianites (v. 4; that
defeat is narrated in Judges 6:1–8:17). All the muddy
boots and bloody uniforms of the enemy will be burned
(v. 5). How is this to take place?

Verse 6 sets it forth. Now it is altogether possible that
in Isaiah's proclamation this verse referred to the birth of
Hezekiah. As it stands, it certainly sounds like a birth
announcement. But there is another possibility, perhaps
even more likely, one that would not necessarily occur to
a modern hearer. That is that it was the announcement,
not of Hezekiah's birth, but of his coronation at the age
of twenty-five (2 Kings 18:2). In the ancient Near East it
was understood that a king, on his coming to the throne,
became a son of the god who sponsored the king. This
appears to have been the context of Psalm 2: we note
there vv. 6–7, where God says, "I have set my king on
Zion, my holy hill," and "You are my son; today I have
begotten you." Indeed Isaiah 9:6 seems to embody the
new king's throne names, affirmations about God: "God
Almighty is a Wonderful Counselor, the Everlasting Father
is Prince of Peace."

Whether this extravagant formula was pronounced
on the birth of Hezekiah, or on his coronation, or on an

occasion for another king of Judah, it not only outlasted the king of Judah over whom Isaiah pronounced it, but it outlasted the Davidic dynasty in Judah altogether. After the destruction of Jerusalem in 587 BCE the passage became a nucleus for the Jewish expectation of the reestablishment of Davidic kingship, a reestablishment that never took place. It is therefore not surprising that we Christians, who understand Jesus to be our Messianic king, who will rule "from this time onward and forevermore," have taken the passage to mark Jesus' birth.

There is a parallel passage, 11:1–10, heard in Advent.[11] The first nine verses fall into two sections—the first (vv. 1–5) describes a just king:

(1)   A shoot shall come out from the stump of Jesse,
        and a branch shall grow out of his roots.

(2)   The spirit of the LORD shall rest on him,
        the spirit of wisdom and understanding,
        the spirit of counsel and might,
        the spirit of knowledge and the fear of the
        LORD.

(3)   His delight shall be in the fear of the LORD.
        He shall not judge by what his eyes see,
        or decide by what his ears hear;

(4)   but with righteousness he shall judge the poor,
        and decide with equity for the meek of the earth;
        he shall strike the earth with the rod of his mouth,
        and with the breath of his lips he shall kill the
        wicked.

(5)   Righteousness shall be the belt around his waist,
        and faithfulness the belt around his loins.

Here is a description of an utterly fair king, a king who will bring social justice back to the realm, who finally will favor the poor and the meek. Did Isaiah have a specific

king in mind? Did these words, along with 9:2–7, originally pertain to Hezekiah? We wonder.

This description of just kingship was cherished by
Jews in later centuries, and it offered for Christians a symbolic description of Jesus Christ, the king forever who
taught that the meek will inherit the earth (Matthew 5:5).

Then the next four verses of Isaiah 11 veer off in a
different direction:

> (6)   The wolf shall live with the lamb,
>   the leopard shall lie down with the kid,
>   the calf and the lion and the fatling together,
>   and a little child shall lead them.
>
> (7)   The cow and the bear shall graze,
>   their young shall lie down together;
>   and the lion shall eat straw like the ox.
>
> (8)   The nursing child shall play over the hole of the asp,
>   and the weaned child shall put its hand on the
>   adder's den.
>
> (9)   They will not hurt or destroy
>   on all my holy mountain;
>   for the earth will be full of the knowledge of the LORD
>   as the waters cover the sea.

Here is a description of the peaceable kingdom. Many
scholars have thought that these verses were heard with
vv. 1–5 from the start, part of the original word of Isaiah
about the just king. Given the shift in subject matter and
the similarity of these verses to the parallel in 65:25, part
of a later layer in the book of Isaiah, I join with other
scholars in concluding that what we have here is an extension drafted two centuries later (accordingly, I shall postpone a discussion of vv. 6–9 until Chapter 6). It only
remains to say that v. 10 is likewise a later addition.

In Chapter 2 and in the present chapter we have surveyed the words of the original Isaiah on Assyria and his
glimpses of hope for the future. In Chapters 4 and 5 we
shall explore the words of the great Second Isaiah. This
treatment leaves several passages in our lectionaries hang-
ing, passages that were evidently drafted after the original
Isaiah but before the Second Isaiah. The most important
among these is 2:1–5 ("swords into plowshares"), which,
as I have said, I shall discuss at the beginning of Chapter
4. There are several others that stand at the edges of various lectionaries, which I shall simply mention here. There
is 30:18–21, part of a promise for YAHWEH's ultimate salvation that probably took shape during the Babylonian
exile (the middle of the sixth century BCE);[12] 32:15–18,
20, covers part of a prophecy of the pouring out of the
Spirit in a time to come, a passage that could have originated either in the seventh or sixth centuries BCE;[13]
33:13–16, gives part of a prophetic liturgy that seems to
have taken shape in the same period;[14] and 38:10–14,
17–20, sets out part of a psalm of thanksgiving attributed
to King Hezekiah in his illness but which is probably a
composition from several decades later.[15]

We have come a long way in Chapters 2 and 3. We
attempted to bring to life the words of the original Isaiah.
We were particularly struck by the way the brutal policies
of Assyria figured in his oracles, indeed by the way he
shaped a theology adequate for international relations.
The specificities of those oracles would fade in later centuries as ebbed and flowed various empires and nations
within the purview of the Old Testament people. Assyrian power, seemingly so invincible at the end of the eighth
century BCE, collapsed at the end of the subsequent century to be replaced by the power of Babylon; and Babylonian power in turn, seemingly so invincible when

Jerusalem fell in 587 BCE and its leaders were marched off to exile in Babylon, collapsed before the expanding Persian empire in 538. The Persian king allowed the Jewish exiles to repatriate Jerusalem, but those who returned saw a shrunken city. Its defense walls were not rebuilt until almost another century had passed, and, the Davidic monarchy was never reinstituted.

Isaiah's theology, then, predicated on an intact Jerusalem and on a monarchy to be purified, inevitably receded in the face of the fresh concerns of Second Isaiah and his followers, concerns that we shall explore in the next three chapters. Of course it was altogether natural that the theology of the original Isaiah should be reconceived as the centuries passed, but it is nevertheless a gain for us today to reconstruct what we can of the message of one of the towering giants of the Old Testament.

NOTES

1. Note that 7:10–14 is also the Old Testament lesson in all the lectionaries for the Feast of the Annunciation (March 25), and in the Roman Catholic weekday lectionary for December 20.

2. This verse leads the hearer so far from Matthew's focus that two of the lectionaries exclude this verse altogether from the reading. In the Revised Common Lectionary the reading is vv. 10–16; in the Roman Catholic lectionary it is vv. 10–14. In the Lutheran lectionary the passage is given as vv. 10–14 with vv. 15–17 as an optional addition. Only in the Episcopal lectionary is the full passage appointed, vv. 10–17.

3. Verses 10–17 are found in our lectionaries, at least in part; curiously, vv. 1–9 occur separately the Roman Catholic weekday lectionary. Isaiah 7:1–9 is the Old Testament lesson in the Roman Catholic lectionary for Tuesday between July 12–18 in Year II.

4. A standard commentary, Hans Wildberger, *Isaiah 1–12* (Minneapolis: Augsburg, 1991), 279, states, "Because of the abundance of the literature which has appeared concerning this section, no effort has been made to cite it in its entirety"; the work then goes on to offer

three full pages of citations to literature that appeared before 1979.

5. For the outline of this sequence of suggestions see Christoph Dohmen, "*almâ*," in G. Johannes Botterweck, et al. *Theological Dictionary of the Old Testament* 11 (Grand Rapids: Eerdmans, 2001), 157, 160–62; and, in more detail, Christoph Dohmen, "Verstockungsvollzug und prophetische Legitimation: Literarkritische Beobachtungen zu Jes 7, 1–17," *Biblische Notizen* 31 (1986), 37–55.

6. For the text see James B. Pritchard, *Ancient Near Eastern Texts Relating to the Old Testament* (Princeton: Princeton University Press, 1995), 288. One of several copies of the text is an inscription in the Oriental Institute of the University of Chicago.

7. Isaiah 10:5–7, 13–16 is the first reading in the Roman Catholic weekday lectionary for the Wednesday from July 13 to 19 in Year II.

8. Verses 15 and 19–23 is the Old Testament lesson in the Roman Catholic lectionary for the Sunday between August 21 and 27 in Year A.

9. It is the Old Testament lesson for the Sunday between August 21 to 27 in Year C.

10. Beyond the omission in the Episcopal lectionary of v. 5, it is to be noted that vv. 1–4 are heard in several traditions during the Epiphany season as well: they are the Old Testament lesson for the Sunday between January 21 and 27 in Year A in the Revised Common Lectionary and in the Roman Catholic Lectionary, but not in the Episcopal lectionary. And I repeat a detail I noted in the Introduction, namely that in Roman Catholic and Jewish translations the *numeration* of these verses is 1–6 rather than 2–7.

11. It is appointed in the lectionaries for the Second Sunday of Advent in the Year A; it is also the Old Testament lesson in the Roman Catholic daily lectionary for the Tuesday of the First Week of Advent.

12. It is the first reading for the festival of Sts. Philip and James, May 1, in the Episcopal and Lutheran lectionaries.

13. In the Roman Catholic lectionary the passage is an alternative reading for the Mass for Independence Day in the United States (July 4) and the Mass for Peace and Justice.

14. It is the canticle for Roman Catholic morning prayer for Wednesday in Week III.

15. It is the canticle for Roman Catholic morning prayer for Holy Saturday, for Tuesday in Week II, and for the Office of the Dead.

Chapter 4 ————————————————

God Will Bring the
Exiles Home

IN CHAPTER 40 OF ISAIAH there begin sixteen chapters of the most awesome sequence of good news to be found anywhere in the Old Testament. Chapter 40 begins, "Comfort, O comfort my people, says your God," and chapter 55 ends with "For you shall go out in joy, and be led back in peace" (v. 12 there). As we have seen, the material in the first thirty-nine chapters seems jittery and changeable, so that, in working through it, we feel the constant need of guidance and commentary, but with chapter 40 we seem able to read without the need of any explanation. In these chapters one feels one can simply read and read and read, taking in more hope with each sequence.

And it is easy to see how these words of hope speak to Christians directly. Many years ago there was a deaconess in a church I served who used to say, "I just love the book of Isaiah." She was a widow in her sixties, crippled with arthritis, and she was nursing her widowed mother. She was a fine example of those who hear Scripture the first way: *Isaiah was talking about us.* And the words of Isaiah spoke directly to her.

I knew when she spoke this way about Isaiah that she did not mean those terrible pronouncements of judgment that we find in the first part of the book (see Chapter 2). No, she meant the words from this latter section of the book that begin, "Comfort, O comfort my people." And the people who had a hand in shaping our lectionaries have chosen just as that deaconess did. Of the 333 verses in Isaiah 40–55, the Revised Common Lectionary includes 102 of them, and the Episcopal lectionary 107.

The deaconess in my church did not need to learn the historical details of the passages of Isaiah, but I suggest that those details can help us. Thus we move to the second way to hear Scripture, asking, as we did with the original Isaiah, what was the historical context of these words. Why were the words of the original Isaiah extended to include this message of glowing hope?

Before we turn to chapters 40–55, however, we need to make a short detour. As I observed in Chapter 1, the book of Isaiah, like other biblical books, underwent expansion from time to time. Disciples and followers of the original prophet collected material considered to have come from the master or to be in the spirit of the master. As I remarked at the end of Chapter 3, even within Isaiah 1–39 one finds a good many additions and expansions that originated in the decades after the prophet himself had passed from the scene.

A prime example of such an expansion in Isaiah 2:1–5, found in all the lectionaries for the First Sunday of Advent in Year A.

(1)   The word that Isaiah son of Amoz saw concerning
      Judah and Jerusalem.

(2)   In days to come
          the mountain of the LORD's house
      shall be established as the highest of the mountains,
          and shall be raised above the hills;
      all the nations shall stream to it.

(3)   Many peoples shall come and say,
      "Come, let us go up to the mountain of LORD,
          to the house of the God of Jacob;
      that he may teach us his ways
          and that we may walk in his paths."
      For out of Zion shall go forth instruction,
          and the word of the LORD from Jerusalem.

(4)   He shall judge between the nations,
          and shall arbitrate for many peoples;
      they shall beat their swords into plowshares,
          and their spears into pruning hooks;
      nation shall not lift up sword against nation,
          neither shall they learn war any more.

(5)   O house of Jacob,
          come, let us walk
          in the light of the LORD!

Verse 1 is a superscription, an editorial note that appears
at the head of a collection of biblical material. Though
there are scholars that assume vv. 2–5 to be genuine to
the original Isaiah, I side with those who understand the
poem to be an anonymous oracle from the sixth century
BCE. It is striking that it is also found in a slightly different form in Micah 4:1–4. It shares with genuine material from Isaiah the notion of the centrality of Jerusalem
(see Chapter 3). The author of the passage envisages the
city not simply transformed into righteousness, but in a
marvelous way becoming the very center of the world ("the

highest of the mountains"). All nations shall come to Jerusalem to learn the ways of God, ways that include international peace.

The extension—and transformation—of the message of Isaiah represented by the material in chapters 40–55 (and more, I believe), is massive. Evidently, this transformation took place about two centuries after Isaiah's time and hundreds of miles to the east, in Babylon. An utterly fresh voice put aside the master's biting message of judgment on the people who neglected social justice and spurned hope shaped by a purified kingship and a purified Jerusalem. Instead the disciple offered a vision of an utterly fresh beginning to his despondent fellow-exiles.

Yet it is hard to know how to bring the author of these chapters to life, because even though scholars have isolated their time and circumstance, the personality of their author remains hidden. If the biographical details of the original Isaiah are few, the biographical details of this successor-prophet are missing altogether. If this prophet's words are stunning, nevertheless his name is reduced to the alias that scholars employ to refer to him— Second Isaiah or, using the Greek prefix, "Deutero-Isaiah". What is more, scholars continue to debate the details of this prophet's activity. Even though the details of these controversies would only impede a presentation here, it is only fair to warn readers that somewhat different reconstructions of Second Isaiah's transforming work are possible.

First a word about the alias. Mark Twain, in his usual tongue-in-cheek manner, once remarked that he had given the question of the authorship of Shakespeare's plays a great deal of thought and had come to the conclusion that the plays were not written by William Shakespeare at all but by another man of the same name. By the same token I have sometimes allowed myself to wonder whether the prophet responsible for Isaiah 40–55 was not also named Isaiah—after all, there are six other people in the Old Testament who carry the name.[1] One might even spin out a scenario of a young man who, having been given this name by his parents, was moved to entertain the vocation of a prophet by the example of his namesake. But of course, for all this, there is not a shred of evidence.

Next, a word about the extent of Second Isaiah's proclamations. There is general agreement that he is responsible for chapters 40–55. I am inclined, along with some scholars, to attribute to him chapter 35 and chapters 56–66 as well. To keep things simple I shall take this tack in the present work. I shall discuss chapter 35 at the end of the present chapter and chapters 56–66 at the end of Chapter 6.

There is a further step, suggested in recent years by the British scholar Hugh Williamson, which I myself favor. That is that Second Isaiah not only proclaimed hundreds of verses of fresh material but was also responsible for a modest *rearrangement* of the material of the original Isaiah, the better to reflect his own understanding of the shape of God's fresh message.

I shall not take account of the details of Williamson's reconstruction, but the reader might be curious to examine an example of what may have taken place (and if he or she is not, the rest of the present paragraph can be skipped!). As we have already noted, 2:1 is a superscription, a circumstance suggesting that at some period chapter 2 marks the beginning of the collection of Isaiah material. The existence of 1:1, *another* superscription, may suggest that chapter 1 is made up of a short, introductory anthology of Isaiah's material, gathered from elsewhere in the collection. Here highlighted as a counterweight to Second Isaiah's own material. Thus

1:2b–3, which begins, "I reared children and brought them up, but they have rebelled against me," originally could have been located between 30:8 and 9, since v. 9 continues the diction of "rebellious people, faithless children." And 1:4, which begins with the Hebrew word *hoy* "ah" or "woe," could well have stood originally before 5:8, which, as it now stands, is the first of a series of parallel pronouncements beginning with that expression. Finally, the bleak picture of the dereliction of daughter Zion after battle in 1:5–9, would have fit well after 30:17, which offers a similar pictures. These suggestions at least open possibilities for us of how Second Isaiah may have shaped the message of his predecessor.[2]

I have already indicated that the Second Isaiah's audience consisted of his fellow exiles in Babylon, so we need to understand his circumstances, which were so very different from those of the first Isaiah. At the end of Chapter 3, I indicated that the Babylonians had taken captive to Babylon the leading citizens of Jerusalem. There were several thousand of them. By 540 BCE a fresh shift of power loomed, for two years later, in 538, from farther east, on the Iranian plateau, King Cyrus of Persia marched west to conquer Babylon and eventually decreed the freedom of the exiles to return to Jerusalem. Evidently it was in this situation of promise that the new prophet spoke out. The exilic community had endured almost a half-century away from their traditional home. A new generation was grown, and few among them could remember Jerusalem at all.

The message of this prophet is broad and massive. In a way it is the center of gravity of the whole Old Testament. Accordingly, we shall spend three chapters of this study on the material. In this chapter we shall concentrate on the news that the exiles will return to Jerusalem

by the intervention of Cyrus, king of Persia. In Chapter
5 we shall examine affirmations that God is the utterly
incomparable Creator. And in Chapter 6 we will take
account of the call of the Suffering Servant and then look
at the material in Isaiah 56–66, where later words of the
prophet appear to be found.

First, then, we turn to the beginning of Second Isaiah's oracles, 40:1–11, the reading for the Second Sunday of Advent in Year B.[3]

> (1) Comfort, O comfort my people,
>   says your God.
>
> (2) Speak tenderly to Jerusalem,
>   and cry to her
>   that she has served her term,
>   that her penalty is paid,
>   that she has received from the LORD's hand
>   double for all her sins.
>
> (3) A voice cries out:
>   "In the wilderness prepare the way of the LORD,
>   make straight in the desert a highway for our God.
>
> (4) Every valley shall be lifted up,
>   and every mountain and hill be made low;
>   The uneven ground shall become level,
>   and the rough places a plain.
>
> (5) Then the glory of the Lord shall be revealed,
>   and all people shall see it together,
>   for the mouth of the Lord has spoken."
>
> (6) A voice says, "Cry out!"
>   And I said, "What shall I cry?"
>   All people are grass,
>   their constancy is like the flower of the field.
>
> (7) The grass withers, the flower fades,
>   when the breath of the LORD blows upon it;
>   surely the people are grass.

(8) The grass withers, the flower fades;
    but the word of our God will stand forever.

(9) Get you up to a high mountain,
    O Zion, herald of good tidings;
lift up your voice with strength,
    O Jerusalem, herald of good tidings,
    lift it up, do not fear;
say to the cities of Judah,
    "Here is your God!"

(10) See, the Lord GOD comes with might,
    and his arm rules for him;
his reward is with him,
    and his recompense before him.

(11) He will feed his flock like a shepherd;
    he will gather the lambs in his arms,
and carry them in his bosom,
    and gentle lead the mother sheep.

I mentioned Handel's *Messiah* in Chapter 3 in connection with 9:2–7 ("For unto us a child is born"), and now in vv. 1–5 we come upon the words heard in the opening sequences of that work. Again, hard though it is, we try to lay aside that music long enough to hear these words freshly, as the exiles did. We hear first the bold expression of a new beginning, a command, perhaps to the heavenly host, "Comfort, O comfort my people." It is worth noting that the Hebrew verb translated "comfort" is related to the word for mother-love. Though in v. 2 the meaning "tenderly" is dear to us, the expression means rather "encouragingly, convincingly."[4] "Jerusalem," that is, the people in exile, "has served her term." In fact, says the prophet, we can think of the forty-seven years or so, just passed, as a term twice as long as justified, but that is all behind us.

It is behind us, because a straight highway will be cut across the desert (vv. 3–4). His listeners wonder: Will

the highway enable us to go home? We are not sure. It
is a highway for "our God," but God is certainly not
earthbound. So why then a highway? Is it for us? We
shall see.

"Then the glory of the LORD shall be revealed" (v.
5). Here is a reminder that this new prophet is a wor-
thy successor to the original Isaiah, because he recalls
that prophet hearing the words of the seraphs, "The
whole earth is full of his glory" (6:3). In v. 6, in the
expression "I said," we have the merest glimpse of the
prophet himself. And what does he proclaim? That even
though human beings are a transitory as grass (something of which his audience hardly needed to be
reminded), God's word, God's covenant and promises,
stand forever (vv. 6–8).

Verses 9–11 shift direction; Jerusalem is addressed.[5]
Since in Hebrew cities are grammatically feminine, and
since Hebrew has grammatical markers for verbs and
pronouns in the second person as well as in the third,
the feminine forms here are startling and refreshing.
Zion, the mount on which the Temple was built, is itself
told to get up onto a high mountain. Is this an echo of
the height of that mount described in 2:2? Zion is to
speak, to announce the arrival of God (v. 9), presumably
in Jerusalem. Again, was that highway (v. 3) for God?
God is certainly pictured as coming like a conquering
hero, with might (v. 10) and "his reward is with him."
The prophet's hearers to wonder, "Are *we* that reward?"
A conquering hero will be in the vanguard of his army.
On the other hand a shepherd (v. 11) stays behind his
sheep, to keep them moving along: "lambs" and "mother
sheep" certainly sound like metaphors for the covenant
people. So in the double image, God is by implication
both leading and following his charges. What food for
thought!

Verses 21–31 of this chapter are designated in all the lectionaries for the Sunday between February 4 and 10 in Year B:[6]

(21) Have you not known? Have you not heard?
   Has it not been told you from the beginning?
   Have you not understood from the foundations
   of the earth?

(22) It is he who sits above the circle of the earth,
   and its inhabitants are like grasshoppers;
 who stretches out the heavens like a curtain,
   and spreads them like a tent to live in;

(23) who brings princes to naught,
   and makes the rulers of the earth as nothing.

(24) Scarcely are they planted, scarcely sown,
   scarcely has their stem taken root in the earth,
 when he blows upon them, and they wither,
   and the tempest carries them off like stubble.

(25) To whom then will you compare me,
   or who is my equal? Says the Holy One.

(26) Lift up your eyes on high and see:
   Who created these?
 He who brings out their host and numbers them,
   calling them all by name;
 because he is great in strength,
   mighty in power,
   not one is missing.

(27) Why do you say, O Jacob,
   and speak, O Israel,
 "My way is hidden from the LORD,
   and my right is disregarded by my God"?

(28) Have you not known? Have you not heard?
 The LORD is the everlasting God,
   the Creator of the ends of the earth.
 He does not faint or grow weary,
   his understanding is unsearchable.

(29) He gives power to the faint,
> and strengthens the powerless.

(30) Even youths will faint and be weary,
> and the young will fall exhausted;

(31) but those who wait for the LORD shall renew their
strength,
> they shall mount up with wings like eagles,
> they shall run and not be weary,
> they shall walk and not faint.

In this sequence we twice hear the rhetorical question, "Have you not known? Have you not heard?" (vv. 21, 28).7 Of course the audience should know of the Creator, who sits above the circle of the earth, v. 22. Recall that the original Isaiah saw God sitting on a *throne*, 6:1— is this an echo of the reference to Zion on a high mountain, v. 9? Indeed it is the Creator of the very ends of the earth (v. 28). This is the God of action, who brings princes to naught and makes the rulers of the earth as nothing (v. 23), whose tempest carries them off like stubble (v. 24). Aha, now we understand. We had heard that human beings were like grass (v. 6), but now we realize that the metaphor applies not only to us, but to princes as well, even the princes of Babylon. God gives power to the faint and strengthens the powerless (v. 29). The powerless God has not forgotten—if God remembers the name of every star (v. 26), then God will not only remember the name of his people Jacob (v. 27, by implication) but will give them new power (v. 31).

Verse 31 carries a special set of implications. Those who first heard the words "Mount up with wings like eagles" would be reminded of the affirmation in Exodus 19:4, words of God from the mouth of Moses, "You have seen what I did to the Egyptians, and how I bore you on eagles' wings and brought you to myself." If the hearers have heard hints of a return home (the highway, God's leadership of his troops), here is a stronger hint. God did it before, in the exodus from Egypt, and God will do it again, in an exodus from Babylon. If only they wait for God, they shall walk, indeed run—on that highway, no doubt.

As we read consecutively into chapter 41 we find these indications of homecoming growing stronger and stronger. How will God bring about that homecoming? By rousing an agent, it seems, "a victor from the east" (41:2). Through him God will carry off nations and kings "like dust and driven stubble." Then in 41:25 we hear another reference to the agent, when we hear God speak, "I stirred up one from the north, and he has come . . . . He shall trample on rulers as on mortar." Who is this agent? We must wait till 44:28 and 45:1 to hear his name. (We shall examine 45:1–7 in a moment). It will turn out to be Cyrus king of Persia.

The homecoming of the exiles, only hinted at in chapters 40–41, becomes explicit in 43:1–7, a passage found in a couple of lectionaries:[8]

(1)   But now thus says the Lord,
        he who created you, O Jacob,
        he who formed you, O Israel:
     Do not fear, for I have redeemed you,
        I have called you by name, you are mine.

(2)   When you pass through the waters, I will be with you;
        and through the rivers, they shall not overwhelm
        you;
     when you walk through fire you shall not be burned,
        and the flame shall not consume you.

(3)   For I am the LORD your God,
        the Holy One of Israel, your Savior.

I give Egypt as your ransom,
  Ethiopia and Seba in exchange for you.

(4) Because you are precious in my sight,
       and honored, and I love you,
     I give people in return for you,
       nations in exchange for your life.

(5) Do not fear, for I am with you;
       I will bring your offspring from the east,
       and from the west I will gather you;

(6) I will say to north, "Give them up,"
       And to south, "Do not withhold;
     bring my sons from far away
       and my daughters from the end of the earth—

(7) everyone who is called by my name,
       whom I created for my glory,
       whom I formed and made."

"I have redeemed you" (v. 1), that is, I have bought your freedom, is again a reminder of the rescue from Egypt (compare Exodus 6:6). Whatever ordeal Israel passes through, whether water or fire, God will be with them. The promise takes on historical specificity as the prophet names Egypt, Ethiopia, and Seba, fabulously wealthy nations that Cyrus would be expected to conquer. However wealthy they may be, God will gladly give them up in exchange for liberation of Israel's exiles. Listen to the roll call of these exiles. Those from the four points of the compass, sons and daughters (vv. 5–6), every one, God will gather them up because they are called by the divine name, owned by God (v. 7).

So who is this Cyrus? We turn to 45:1–7, a passage in the Roman Catholic and Episcopal lectionaries,[9] and examine the first five verses:

(1)   Thus says the LORD to his anointed, to Cyrus,
          whose right hand I have grasped
      to subdue nations before him
          and strip kings of their robes,
      to open doors before him—
          and the gates shall not be closed:

(2)   I will go before you
          and level the mountains,
      I will break in pieces the doors of bronze
          and cut through the bars of iron,

(3)   I will give you the treasures of darkness
          and riches hidden in secret places,
      so that you may know that it is I, the LORD,
          the God of Israel, who call you by your name.

(4)   For the sake of my servant Jacob,
          and Israel my chosen,
      I call you by your name,
          I surname you, though you do not know me.

(5)   I am the LORD, and there is no other;
          besides me there is no god.
      I arm you, though you do not know me.

Ancient texts record Cyrus as the king of a territory called
Anshan in southern Iran. In 550 BCE he rose in revolt and
took control of the vast Median empire, which was centered
in northwest Iran but controlled most of what was then
called Persia. But in 540 he was a clear threat to the steadily
weakening Babylonian empire. It was this figure, high on
the Persian plateau to the east of Babylon, "a victor from
the east" (41:2), "one from the north" (41:25), to whom Second Isaiah looked as the means for the coming liberation.

    The prophet gives Cyrus an astonishing title: he is
God's "anointed" (v. 1)—the Hebrew word comes into
English as "Messiah." For forty-seven years the exiles had·
been looking *west*, toward home, toward Jerusalem,

wondering when they could be released to return and enjoy the renewal of the Davidic monarchy. Now, suddenly, they hear that God's new designated one, the king to win their battles for them, will not be of the line of David at all, but rather someone from far to the *east* who does not speak a word of Hebrew. God grasps Cyrus's right hand. Cyrus will "subdue nations" (compare 41:2, 25).

There is a nice balance between vv. 1 and 5 here, a balance that is somewhat fuzzy in translation. In v. 1 the Hebrew phrase for "strip kings of their robes" is literally "the loins of kings I shall open [that is, ungird]," and the Hebrew phrase for "I arm you" (v. 5) is literally "I shall gird you." In Old Testament idiom, in order to fight, one "girds one's loins," that is, tucks the hem of one's robe inside one's girdle (or belt). This frees the legs for action (something like "rolling up one's sleeves"). Thus God renders the kings of Babylon unfit for battle at the same time as Cyrus is made fit for battle.

God addresses Cyrus: "I will go before you" to break down all barriers to victory "so that you may know that it is I, the LORD, the God of Israel, who call you by your name" (vv. 2–3). In the British Museum there is an inscription, the so-called "Cyrus Cylinder," set up after the fall of Babylon. It describes how Marduk, the god of Babylon, "scoured all the lands for a friend, seeking for the upright prince whom it would have to take his hand. He called Cyrus, king of Anshan. He nominated him [literally, 'pronounced (his) name'] to be ruler over all."[10] It is clear, then, that in this passage Second Isaiah is drawing on the standard court language of Babylonia and Persia. It is for the sake of "Israel my chosen," God calls Cyrus by his name and gives him a title ("I surname you," v. 4). What is that title? Evidently "Messiah." We notice (vv. 4–5) that Cyrus does not even know that it is Yahweh who

gives him this title and arms him. In Chapter 3, I cited
10:7, in which the original Isaiah affirmed that Assyria did
not need to know that it was God's agent for the punishment of the covenant people. Now, by the same token,
we hear that Cyrus does not need to know that he is God's
agent in the rescue of the covenant people. Nevertheless,
he is. The prophet continues to refer to Cyrus beyond
chapter 45. We hear in 46:11 that God calls "a bird of
prey from the east, the man for my purpose from a far
country," and in 48:14 that "the LORD loves him [Cyrus];
he shall perform his purpose on Babylon."

The rest of the phrases in 45:5–7 affirm that Yahweh
is altogether unique, the God not only of history but of
creation. I shall return to these topics in Chapter 5, but
for now let us stay with history. In 51:9–11[11] we have an
astonishing sequence of images:

> (9) Awake, awake, put on strength,
>   O arm of the LORD!
>   Awake, as in days of old,
>   the generations of long ago!
>   Was it not you who cut Rahab in pieces,
>   who pierced the dragon?
>
> (10) Was it not you who dried up the sea,
>   the waters of the great deep;
>   who made the depths of the sea a way
>   for the redeemed to cross over?
>
> (11) So the ransomed of the LORD shall return,
>   and come to Zion with singing;
>   everlasting joy shall be upon their heads;
>   they shall obtain joy and gladness,
>   and sorrow and sighing shall flee away.

"Rahab" in v. 9 is a designation of the sea monster in an
old Canaanite myth of a deity victorious in combat with

that monster. In the Canaanite version the fertility god, Baal, was victor, but here the myth accommodates Israel's belief that YAHWEH is victor. Now it is no longer an old myth—now it is *history*, since Yahweh's deliverance of the Israelites from Egypt through the sea has been shaped by the narrative pattern of the old myth. The "arm" of YAH-WEH is the instrument of God's deliverance (Deuteronomy 4:34). We have heard of it before in Second Isaiah (40:11), so we are prepared to hear once more the news of a new exodus: "the ransomed of the LORD shall return, and come to Zion with singing" (v. 11).

The four verses of 52:7–10 are heard among the lections for Christmas.[12] A messenger comes over one mountain after another to announce "peace," "good news," and "salvation" to Jerusalem, "the return of the LORD to Zion." It is a glorious message.

One theme, repeated again and again, is the reassurance to Israel, "Do not fear." We have already met this phrase in 40:9 and in 43:1 and 5. It is found again in 41:13 and 14,[13] in 44:8,[14] and in 54:4. The wording is similar here in 41:14.[15]

One reason the prophet's hearers are not to fear is the news that on the homeward journey no one will be thirsty, for God will bring water and make the desert bloom. The dearth of water in the desert must have made a deep impression on those who were forced to journey to Babylon in 587, for the prophet affirms the word again and again. We have mentioned 41:13–20 and 44:1–8 in connection with "do not fear." Let us look now at 41:17–20:[16]

> (17) When the poor and needy seek water,
>   and there is none,
>   and their tongue is parched with thirst,
>   I the LORD will answer them,
>   I the God of Israel will not forsake them.

(18) I will open rivers on the bare heights,
     and fountains in the midst of the valleys;
  I will make the wilderness a pool of water,
     and the dry land springs of water.

(19) I will put in the wilderness the cedar,
     the acacia, the myrtle, and the olive;
  I will set in the desert the cypress,
     the plane and the pine together,

(20) that all may see and know,
     all may consider and understand,
  That the hand of the LORD has done this,
     the Holy One of Israel has created it.

During the first exodus, out of Egypt, God brought water out of the rock (see Exodus 17; Isaiah 48:21 refers to it). It will happen again in the next exodus. The desert will become an oasis. The theme is found again in 43:19–20;[17] 49:10;[18] and 51:3.[19]

Though chapter 35 of Isaiah falls outside the boundaries of the chapters normally assigned to Second Isaiah, it gives every evidence of coming from him:[20]

(1) The wilderness and the dry land shall be glad,
     the desert shall rejoice and blossom;
  like the crocus it shall blossom abundantly,
     and rejoice with joy and singing.
  The glory of Lebanon shall be given to it,
     the majesty of Carmel and Sharon.
  They shall see the glory of the LORD,
     the majesty of our God.

(3) Strengthen the weak hands,
     and make firm the feeble knees.

(4) Say to those who are of a fearful heart,
     "Be strong, do not fear!
  Here is Your God.
     He will come with vengeance,

                 with terrible recompense.
                 He will come and save you."

    (5)   Then the eyes of the blind shall be opened,
              and the ears of the deaf unstopped;

    (6)   then the lame shall leap like a deer,
              and the tongue of the speechless sing for joy.
          For waters shall break forth in the wilderness,
              and streams in the desert;

    (7)   the burning sand shall become a pool,
              and the thirsty ground spring of water;
          the haunt of jackals shall become a swamp,
              the grass shall become reeds and rushes.

    (8)   A highway shall be there,
              and it shall be called the Holy Way;
          the unclean shall not travel on it,
              but it shall be for God's people;
              no traveler, not even fools, shall go astray.

    (9)   No lion shall be there,
              nor shall any ravenous beast come up on it;
          they shall not be found there,
              but the redeemed shall walk there.

    (10) And the ransomed of the LORD shall return,
              and come to Zion with singing;
          everlasting joy shall be upon their heads;
              they shall obtain joy and gladness,
          and sorrow and sighing shall flee away.

Here are themes we have already encountered: the blooming desert (vv. 1–2, 7), the reassurance "do not fear" (v.
4), the highway for God's people (v. 8), the joyful return
to Zion (v. 10). No wonder the deaconess in my church
loved Isaiah! The words spoke to her directly, without any
historical specificity. This elevated language, suitable for
metaphor, can bring hope and joy directly into the heart
of any believer.

We have touched on related themes of Second
Isaiah—that the God of Israel is Creator, and unique.
These are the themes we shall explore in the next chapter.

NOTES

1. In these instances the NRSV gives the name as "Jeshaiah," but
it is the same name in Hebrew. In Ezra 8:19, for example, a Jeshaiah is listed as among those who returned with Ezra to Jerusalem
about 450 BCE.

2. Hugh G. M. Williamson, "Relocating Isaiah 1:2–9," Craig C.
Broyles and Craig A. Evans, *Writing and Reading the Scroll of Isaiah,
Studies of an Interpretive Tradition* (Supplements to Vetus Testamen-
tum 70; Leiden: E. J. Brill, 1997), 263–77.

3. The Roman Catholic Lectionary for that Sunday omits vv. 6–8,
but in its Weekday Lectionary, in the first reading for Tuesday of the
second week of Advent, all eleven verses are included. One notes also
that the Episcopal lectionary uses vv. 1–11 for the feast of the Nativ-
ity of John the Baptist, June 24.

4. Karl Elliger, *Deuterojesaja*, Teilband 1 (Biblischer Kommentar
Altes Testament 11; Neukirchen: Neukirchener Verlag, 1978), 13.

5. Though vv. 9–11 are part of some lections (see note 3), at the
same time vv. 10–17 are a canticle occurring in morning prayer of
Thursday in Week III in the Roman Catholic liturgy of the hours.

6. And the Roman Catholic Weekday Lectionary uses vv. 25–31 for
the Wednesday of the Second Week of Advent.

7. For variety's sake the Hebrew verb forms are slightly different, in
the two verses, but the translation is not affected.

8. These verses are set forth in the Revised Common Lectionary
for the Feast of the Baptism of the Lord (the First Sunday After the
Epiphany, the Sunday between January 7 and 13) in Year C, but the
other lectionaries do not use this passage. The Episcopal lectionary
offers 43:1–12 as an alternative reading for the Third Sunday of
Easter in Year A.

9. It is the Old Testament reading in the Roman Catholic, Episcopal, and Lutheran lectionaries for the Sunday between October 16
and 22 in Year A, though the Roman Catholic reading omits vv. 2–3
and 7. The Roman Catholic Weekday Missal further designates the

last line of v. 6 and all of vv. 7–8, 18, 21–25 for the Wednesday of the Third Week of Advent.

10. D. Winton Thomas (ed.), *Documents from Old Testament Times* (London/New York: Thomas Nelson and Sons, 1958), 92; compare James Pritchard (ed.), *Ancient Near Eastern Texts Relating to the Old Testament* (Princeton: Princeton University Press, 1955), 315.

11. An alternative Old Testament lesson in the Episcopal lectionary for the Principal Service for Easter Day in Year C.

12. It is the Old Testament lesson associated with the Gospel reading from John 1:1–14. It is set forth in the Revised Common Lectionary as part of a second set of alternative lections for Christmas eve or Christmas day; in the Roman Catholic lectionary it is part of the lections for the Mass on Christmas day; in the Episcopal lectionary it is part of the lections for the third service of Christmas day; and in the Lutheran lectionary it is part of the lections for the second service of Christmas day. For Episcopalians and Lutherans it is also the Old Testament passage for the Feast of St. Mark (April 25). One notes that the passage is also chosen for the common of a missionary, part of the first set of suggested lections in the Episcopal lectionary, and as an alternative reading outside the Easter season in the Roman Catholic lectionary.

13. The Roman Catholic Weekday Lectionary uses 41:13–20 for Thursday of the Second Week of Advent. It also uses vv. 8–10, 13–14 as an alternative reading in the Mass for persecuted Christians.

14. The Episcopal lectionary suggests 44:1–8 as an alternative Old Testament reading for Pentecost in Year B, and the Lutheran lectionary uses vv. 6–8 for the Sunday between July 17 and 23 in Year A. In addition the Roman Catholic lectionary sets vv. 1–3 as an alternative reading for Christian initiation apart from the Easter Vigil.

15. The Roman Catholic lectionary sets forth 54:5–14 for the Fourth Old Testament Reading for the Easter Vigil, and 54:1–10 in their Weekday Lectionary for Thursday in the Third Week of Advent.

16. Beyond the use of 41:13–20 in the Roman Catholic Weekday Lectionary (see note13), it is to be noted that 41:17–20 is an alternative reading in the Episcopal lectionary for the Sixth Sunday of Easter in Year A.

17. These verses are found in two lectionary sequences: 43:16–21 for the Fifth Sunday in Lent in Year C in all the lectionaries, and 43:18–25 for the Sunday between February 18 and 24 in Year B in all the lectionaries (though the Roman Catholic lectionary omits vv. 20 and 23 there).

18. The Episcopal lectionary calls for 49:8–18, and the Revised Common Lectionary for 49:8–16a, for the Sunday between February 25 and 19 (in a year with late Easter), or for the Sunday between May 24 and 28 (in a year with early Easter), in Year A. But on the occasion of the Sunday between February 25 and March 1 the Roman Catholic lectionary uses only vv. 14–15, thus omitting the verse referring to water in the desert. The Roman Catholic Weekday Lectionary further uses 49:8–15 for the Wednesday of the Fourth Week in Lent.

19. The Episcopal and Lutheran lectionaries use 51:1–6 for the Sunday between August 21 and 27 in Year A.

20. Some scholars have suggested that Second Isaiah used this chapter to unite the collection of words of the original Isaiah with his own words; see Hugh G. M. Williamson, *The Book Called Isaiah, Deutero-Isaiah's Role in Composition and Redaction* (Oxford: Clarendon Press, 1994), 211–16. The entire chapter is the Old Testament reading in the Revised Common Lectionary for the Third Sunday of Advent in Year A; the Roman Catholic lectionary uses vv. 1–6 and 10 for that Sunday. In addition, the Roman Catholic Weekday Lectionary uses the entire chapter for the Monday of the Second Week of Advent.

Chapter 5 ───────────────

God is Creator, the Incomparable

IN OUR DISCUSSION OF 40:21–31 in Chapter 4 we took note of the theme of YAHWEH as Creator God, and it is a theme that recurs again and again in the prophet's words. In the belief system of present-day Christians this theme is basic. We are surrounded by scientific discoveries, and we take for granted the creative work of God. It comes as something of a surprise to perceive how distinctive this theme is in Second Isaiah. We must understand that before the Babylonian exile the focus of Israel's faith was not so much on *creation* as on the *covenant* with YAHWEH. When the Jews were exiled in Babylon, however, one has the impression that one of the few familiar elements that remained was the same stars in the night sky that they had always known. Second Isaiah argues from the familiarity of the stars to the affirmation that God has numbered those stars, called them all by name (40:26), indeed is responsible for the whole created world.

Chapter 45 offers a whole array of such affirmations.[1] In v. 7 we hear, "I form light and created darkness, I make weal and create woe; I the LORD do all these things." In v. 12, "I made the earth, and created humankind upon it; it was my hand that stretched out the heavens, and I commanded all their host." Because YAHWEH is the Creator of the heavens and the earth, it follows that there is no other god. It may surprise us that in earlier periods of Israel's history many people took it for granted that if YAHWEH was the God of Israel, there were other gods of other nations, too. Traces of these beliefs were mostly excluded from the Old Testament, as one might imagine, but there are traces. For example, in Judges 11:24 Jephthah the Gileadite, in addressing the Ammonites, speaks of the land that the god Chemosh (the god of the Moabites) gave to his hearers and of the land that the LORD (YAHWEH) gave to Israel, as if each deity gave out appropriate territory to the respective client of that deity. Earlier prophets moved Israel away from such notions. We saw in Chapter 3 how the original Isaiah proclaimed that it was YAHWEH who was moving Assyria against Israel and Judah.

Second Isaiah gave the deathblow to any lingering notion of the existence of other gods. Again in chapter 45, v. 6 affirms, "I am the LORD, there is no other," and in v. 18 we hear, "For thus says the LORD, who created the heavens (he is God!), whoformed the earth and made it (he established it; he did not create it a chaos, he formed it to be inhabited!): I am the LORD, and there is no other."

If YAHWEH is the only God, then those folk who worship other gods are on the wrong track altogether. Look at 43:8–13.[2]

(8) Bring forth the people who are blind, yet have eyes,
        who are deaf, yet have ears!

(9) Let all the nations gather together,
        and let the peoples assemble.
     Who among them declared this,
        and foretold to us the former things?
     Let them bring their witnesses to justify them,
        and let them hear and say, "It is true."

(10) You are my witnesses, says the LORD,
        and my servant whom I have chosen,
     so that you may know and believe me
        and understand that I am he.
     Before me no god was formed,
        nor shall there be any after me.

(11) I, I am the LORD,
        and besides me there is no savior.

(12) I declared and saved and proclaimed,
        when there was no strange god among you;
        and you are my witnesses, saying the LORD.

(13) I am God, and also henceforth I am He;
        there is no one who can deliver from my hand;
        I work and who can hinder it?

The nations are blind and deaf, while Israel is witness to
the only true God.

Indeed the nations will be shamed and humiliated
once they become aware that their gods are utterly inef-
fective. This is the basic assumption behind the closing
section of chapter 45.[3]

(20) Assemble yourselves and come together,
        draw near, you survivors of the nations!
     They have no knowledge—
        those who carry about their wooden idols,
     and keep on praying to a god
        that cannot save.

(21) Declare and present your case;
  let them take counsel together!
 Who told this long ago?
  Who declared it of old?
 Was it not I, the LORD?
  There is no other god besides me,
 a righteous God and a Savior;
  there is no one besides me.

(22) Turn to me and be saved,
  all the ends of the earth!
 For I am God, and there is no other.

(23) By myself I have sworn,
  from my mouth has gone forth in righteousness
  a word that shall not return:
 "To me every knee shall bow,
  every tongue shall swear."

(24) Only in the LORD, it shall be said of me,
  are righteousness and strength;
 all who were incensed against him
  shall come to him and be ashamed.

(25) In the LORD all the offspring of Israel
  shall triumph and glory.

Here the survivors of other nations are addressed. They carry their idols around (v. 20), what defense can they make (v. 21)? "Only in the LORD, it shall be said of me, are righteousness and strength" (v. 24).

Indeed in the first two verses of chapter 46 (material not heard in any of our lectionaries) two of the gods of Babylon are mocked by name. First Bel (the Babylonian form of Baal), a designation of Marduk, and then the son of Marduk, Nebo (whose name forms part of the name Nebuchadnezzar), are described as "bowing down " and "stooping." Why? Because their images are being tipped over to be hauled away to oblivion. So much for the gods of Israel's conquerors. The mockery of idols and the

stupidity of those who make or worship them is a stock
theme in Second Isaiah. One can list passages with this
theme: 40:18–20; 41:6–7; 42:17; 44:9–20; 45:16; 46:1,
5–7. Strikingly, our lectionaries do not include *any* of
these passages. Evidently it is assumed that, for Christians, idolatry is not a current theme (though this as an
assumption that one might debate).

In any event, it is instructive to look at the longest of
these, 44:9–20, a satire. Though this passage is printed
as prose in most translations, I suggest it is intended as
rough poetry, really *bad* poetry to reflect the bad theology
of idolatry. Accordingly I shall display it as poetry here.[4]

(9)   All who make idols are nothing,
         and the things they delight in do not profit;
      their witnesses neither see nor know.
         And so they will be put to shame.

(10) Who would fashion a god
         or cast an image
         that can do no good?

(11) Look, all its devotees shall be put to shame;
         the artisans too are merely human.
      Let them all assemble, let them stand up;
         they shall be terrified, they shall all be put to
         shame.

(12) The ironsmith fashions it
         and works it over the coals,
      shaping it with hammers,
         and forging it with his strong arm;
      he becomes hungry and his strength fails,
         he drinks no water and is faint.

(13) The carpenter stretches a line,
         marks it out with a stylus,
      fashions it with planes,
         and marks it with a compass;
      he makes it in human form,

with human beauty,
to be set up in a shrine.

(14) He cuts down cedars
or chooses and holm tree or an oak
and lets it grow strong among the trees of the forest.
He plants a cedar
and the rain nourishes it.

(15) Then it can be used as fuel.
Part of it he takes and warms himself;
he kindles a fire and bakes bread.
Then he makes a god and worships it,
makes it a carved image and bows down before it.

(16) Half of it he burns in the fire;
over this half he roasts meat
eats it and is satisfied.
He also warms himself and says,
"Ah, I am warm, I can feel the fire!"

(17) The rest of it he makes into a god, his idol,
bows down to it and worships it;
he prays to it and says,
"Save me, for you are my god!"

(18) They do not know, nor do they comprehend;
for their eyes are shut, so that they cannot see,
and their minds as well, so that they cannot
understand.

(19) No one considers,
nor is there knowledge or discernment to say,
"Half of it I burned in the fire;
I also baked bread on its coals,
I roasted meat and have eaten.
Now shall I make the rest of it an abomination?
Shall I fall down before a block of wood?"

(20) He feeds on ashes;
a deluded mind has led him astray,
and he cannot save himself or say,
"Is not this thing in my right hand a fraud?"

Beyond the obvious message of the passage, that idols are a delusion, I should like to stress three matters. The first is that the joke is told three times. The speaker tells it first in vv. 9–15, with the punch lines—with half he makes a fire, and with half he makes a god. Then he tells the punch lines again in vv. 16–17. Finally, he tells the punch lines a third time in v. 19. It is as if the hearers are too dense to get it the first time round, or the second time either.

The second is that our tour of the idol factory is backwards. We hear of the metal sheathing of the idol (v. 12), then of the working of the wooden core (v. 13), then of cutting down the tree for the core, then of choosing the tree, then of planting it in the first place (v. 14). The third is that the poetry is so sloppy that we sometimes cannot tell whether it is the idols or the idol-makers that are being described. Who is described in v. 18? Idol-makers are blind (v. 9), but so are idols (Psalm 115:5). One becomes like what one worships!

Now there surely must have been Babylonians who could distinguish between a notion of a heavenly deity on the one hand and the image of a deity set up in a temple on the other, but Second Isaiah does not bother with such niceties. Since it was forbidden to make an image of YAHWEH, it was more ironic to mock the confusion between pagan deity and image the confusion between image and image-maker, as he did.

Since the Babylonians were victorious over the defenders of Jerusalem, there surely must have been Babylonians who mocked the Jewish exiles. They probably voiced the ancient equivalent of "Our Marduk is stronger than your YAHWEH," especially given the *size* of the Babylonian images in their temples. Surely there were those, especially young people, who, though Jewish, would be tempted by the Babylonian way of life and content to settle down in Babylon. To all who even looked at idols out of the corner of their eye, Second Isaiah offers this amazing, contemptuous passage. Bad poetry, the punch line heard three times, the backwards tour of the factory, the confusion between the idol-makers and the idols, the whole mind-set of idolatry was upside-down, backwards, confused, and deluded.

There is no comparison with the biblical God! The verses before and after the passage on idolatry make that clear.[5] "Who is like me?" asks God (44:7). The answer is obvious: no one. "I am the first, and I am the last," we read in 44:6 (and in 48:12). In contrast to the witnesses to idolatry (v. 9), the people of Israel are God's witnesses (v. 8). If the idol-maker tries to make a god (vv. 9–20), it is YAHWEH who has made Israel (v. 21), indeed who has made all things (v. 24). If the idol-maker calls on his idol to save him (v. 17), it is YAHWEH who saves Israel (46:4). The first eleven verses of chapter 46 reinforce the theme of the incomparability of YAHWEH.

Not only does Second Isaiah stress the creative activity of God, he underlines the newness of what God has embarked upon. In Chapter 4, we discussed the theme of rivers in the desert, and I mentioned 43:19.[6] Of those rivers God says, "I am about to do a new thing." In the verse just preceding we hear, "Do not remember the former things."

About the "former things" Second Isaiah seems ambivalent. He may say, "do not remember the former things," but then at another point the hearers are commanded to "remember the former things" (46:9, a passage not included in our lectionaries). These "former things" are doubtless God's acts of judgment set forth in the original Isaiah. They were true, they were valid for their time, but we must not fixate on them, because now God is bringing forth in our midst a new set of actions altogether.

The themes of Second Isaiah are nicely summed up in 42:10–16:[7] all the regions of the earth are to "sing to the LORD a new song" (v. 10); YAHWEH once more "goes forth like a soldier." In sum, YAHWEH alone is awesome in all that is created in heaven and earth, in all the events of human history, and in compassion for the covenant people.

I introduced Second Isaiah in Chapter 4 by offering Hugh Williamson's proposal that this prophet had a major share in rearranging the material of the original Isaiah. There is a short chapter early in the book, chapter 12, that closes off the primary collection of material from the original Isaiah (chapters 1–11). This chapter gives every evidence of having been drafted by Second Isaiah,[8] and I cite it here because it figures as a response (that is, as a substitution for the normal Psalm reading), notably in both Advent and the Easter Vigil.[9] Its note is joy (v. 6).

Joy. At the beginning of Chapter 4, I stated that chapters 40–55 comprise sixteen chapters of the most awesome sequence of good news to be found in the Old Testament, and I set side by side the opening verse of chapter 40 and the next-to-last verse of chapter 55. I examined most of chapter 40, and it is appropriate here to examine the whole of chapter 55. Combinations of its thirteen verses are heard on many occasions in our lectionaries, and they are familiar and dear to us.[10]

    (1)   Ho, everyone who thirsts,
           come to the waters;
       and you that have no money,
           come, buy and eat!
       Come, buy wine and milk
           without money and without price.

    (2)   Why do you spend your money for that which is
       not bread,

and your labor for that which does not satisfy?
Listen carefully to me, and eat what is good,
and delight yourselves in rich food.

(3) Incline your ear, and come to me;
listen, so that you may live.
I will make with you an everlasting covenant,
my steadfast, sure love for David.

(4) See, I made him a witness to the peoples,
a leader and commander for the peoples.

(5) See, you shall call nations that you do not know,
and nations that do not know you shall run to you,
because of the LORD your God, the Holy One of
Israel,
for he has glorified you.

(6) Seek the LORD while he may be found,
call upon him while he is near;

(7) let the wicked forsake their way,
and the unrighteous their thoughts;
let them return to the LORD, that he may have
mercy on them,
and to our God, for he will abundantly pardon.

(8) For my thoughts are not your thoughs,
nor are your ways my ways, says the LORD.

(9) For as the heavens are higher than the earth,
so are my ways higher than your ways
and my thoughts than your thoughts.

(10) For as the rain and the snow come down from heaven,
and do not return there until they have watered
the earth,
making it bring forth and sprout,
giving seed to the sower and bread to the eater,

(11) so shall my word be that goes out from my mouth;
it shall not return to me empty,
but it shall accomplish that which I purpose,
and succeed in the thing for which I sent it.

(12) For you shall go out in joy,
     and be led back in peace;
  the mountains and the hills before you
     shall burst into song,
  and all the trees of the field shall clap their hands.

(13) Instead of the thorn shall come up the cypress;
       instead of the brier shall come up the myrtle;
   and it shall be to the LORD for a memorial,
       for an everlasting sign that shall not be cut off.

"Come to the waters!" Here is water once more, and not only water, but food and drink, and all of it free (vv. 1–2). Since Israel does not live by bread alone, but by YAHWEH's word (compare Deuteronomy 8:3), the prophet's hearers are enjoined, "Incline your ear, and come to me; listen, so that you may live" (v. 3a). The word in 40:8, that "the word of God will stand forever," implies that God's covenant with Israel is forever. Now we hear it explicitly, "I will make with you an evarlasting covenant." This covenant was made long ago with David (vv. 3b–4). It was in no way abrogated by the collapse of the monarchy at the fall of Jerusalem, nor was it abrogated even by the approach of YAHWEH new Messiah Cyrus. The nations of the world will honor Israel because of what YAHWEH is doing (v. 5).

Now how would the prophet's hearers have heard vv. 6–9? The word "wicked" in Hebrew also means "guilty," and I suggest that this is the meaning here. Who are these guilty ones? Walter Brueggemann suggests that it is Jews who ignore this good news of YAHWEH, who are content to stay settled in Babylon.[11] It is they who need to seek YAHWEH while there is still the opportunity, before the homeward journey gets under way. Look carefully at the intricate arrangement of the key words "thoughts," "ways," "my," and "your" in vv. 8–9, used to demonstrate in every way how

contrasting YAHWEH's intention is from the intention of
those who hesitate: *"my* thoughts," *"your* thoughts," then,
reversing the order of possessives, *"your* ways," *"my* ways";
then, reversing the order of the nouns, *"my* ways," *"your*
ways," *"my* thoughts," *"your* thoughts." Having established
the distance of heaven from earth in these verses, we now
hear how YAHWEH 's word, like YAHWEH's fructifying rain
and snow (water once more!) connect heaven and earth.
YAHWEH's word is not like an empty echo, going out and
coming back without having accomplished anything. No!
That word is an accomplishing word, a word that succeeds.

   The closing two verses, vv. 12–13, recapitulate and
reinforce many of the themes of which we have heard:
the new exodus, joy and song (51:11), peace (52:7), the
mountains witnessing the great deliverance (40:9; 52:7),
the fertility and land bedecked with trees (41:19), and the
everlastingness of YAHWEH's work (40:8).

   What more do Second Isaiah's hearers need to hear?
Actually there is one thing more, and it is a very great
thing indeed: it is the stunning message of a vocation for
suffering, set forth in the four so-called Servant Songs
(42:1–9; 49:1–7; 50:4–11; and 52:13–53:12). This message, central for both Second Isaiah and for Christians
who read Isaiah, we shall explore in Chapter 6.

NOTES

   1. For the uses of 45:6–7 and 18 in Roman Catholic and Lutheran
lectionaries see Chapter 4, note 9. Further vv. 11–13, 18–19 are an
alternative reading in the Episcopal lectionary for the Sixth Sunday
of Easter in Year B.

   2. This is an alternative reading in the Lutheran lectionary for the
feast of St. Luke, October 18.

   3. In the Episcopal lectionary 45:21–25 make up a reading for Holy
Cross Day and an alternative reading in the Liturgy of the Word for
Palm Sunday. One notes also that vv. 15–25 are the canticle in the

Roman Catholic Liturgy of the Hours for morning prayer for Friday of Week I.

4. It is displayed as poetry in the standard edition of the Hebrew Bible, *Biblia Hebraica Stuttgartensia* (Stuttgart: Deutsche Bibelstiftung, 1967–77), and in *Tanakh: A New Translation of the Holy Scriptures According to the Traditional Hebrew Text* (Philadelphia: Jewish Publication Society, 1985).

5. Isaiah 44:1–8 is an alternative Old Testament reading in the Episcopal lectionary for Pentecost in Year B.

6. See Chapter 4, n. 17.

7. This passage is a canticle in the Roman Catholic Liturgy of the Hours for morning prayer on Monday in Week IV.

8. For a careful discussion of the matter see Hugh G. M. Williamson, *The Book Called Isaiah, Deutero-Isaiah's Role in Composition and Redaction* (Oxford: Clarendon, 1994), 118–23, 154–55.

9. Verses 2–6 serve as the response after the reading of Isaiah 55:1–11 in the Easter Vigil in the Revised Common Lectionary and the Roman Catholic lectionary, and an alternative response at that point in the vigil in the Episcopal lectionary. They likewise serve as the response on the Third Sunday of Advent in Year C in the Revised Common Lectionary and the Roman Catholic lectionary, and an alternative response on that Sunday in the Episcopal lectionary. The whole chapter serves as a response on the Sunday between November 13 and 19 in Year C in the Revised Common Lectionary. One may note also that in the Liturgy of the Hours for Roman Catholics the whole chapter is the canticle for morning prayer for Thursday in Week II, and that vv. 2–6 make up "Canticle 9, The First Song of Isaiah, *Ecce Deus*," an alternative canticle for Morning Prayer in the Episcopal Book of Common Prayer.

10. Verses 1–11 of chapter 55 are the fifth of seven Old Testament lessons at the Easter Vigil. Beyond this reading one notes the following readings. The whole passage is used as the Old Testament lesson in the Episcopal lectionary for a church convention. The Revised Common Lectionary uses vv. 1–9 for the Third Sunday in Lent in Year C. The Revised Common Lectionary, and likewise the Lutheran lectionary, uses vv. 10–13 late in February or late in May in Year C in two rare situations—on the Sunday between February 25 and 29 if that Sunday does not fall within Lent and if that Sunday is not the Transfiguration of the Lord, or on the Sunday between May 24 and 28 when that Sunday falls after Trinity Sunday. In the Episcopal lec-

tionary vv. 1–5 and 10–13 are designated for the Sunday between July 10 and 16 in Year A. In the Lutheran lectionary vv. 1–5 are assigned for the Sunday between July 31 and August 6 in Year A. In the Roman Catholic lectionary on that same Sunday vv. 1–3 are used. Verses 6–9 are used in the Roman Catholic lectionary on the Sunday between September 18 and 24 in Year A, and as an alternative reading in the Mass for Forgiveness of Sins. For the Sunday between July 10 and 16 in Year A vv. 10–13 are assigned in the Lutheran lectionary and vv. 10–11 in the Roman Catholic lectionary; vv. 10–11 are likewise heard in the Roman Catholic Weekday Lectionary on the Tuesday in the First Week in Lent. It is also to be noted that in the Episcopal lectionary vv. 6–11 make up the so-called "Canticle 10, the Second Song of Isaiah, *Quaerite Dominum*," an alternative canticle for Morning Prayer.

11. Walter Brueggemann, *Isaiah 40–66* (Westminster Bible Companion; Louisville, KY: Westminster John Knox, 1998), 160.

The Call to Suffer—
Proclaimed and Ignored

THREE TASKS REMAIN TO US in our discussion of the original context of the material of the book of Isaiah. The first and most important, which we have postponed till now, is to come to terms with the "Servant Songs" within chapters 40–55. The second is to deal with the material in chapters 56–66. The third is to touch on a few passages that were added to the book of Isaiah in the decades after the addition of those eleven chapters. These are the matters for this chapter.

THE SERVANT SONGS: GOD PROMISES TO ACT

Of all the material in Isaiah 40–55 none has attracted more attention than four sequences that are commonly called the "Servant Songs," poems that depict a suffering servant. These passages are 42:1–9; 49:1–7; 50:4–9 and

52:13–53:12.[1] Christians hear them at crucial points in the church year: 42:1–9 is heard on the occasion of the Baptism of the Lord (that is, the First Sunday after the Epiphany) and on Monday in Holy Week.[2] 49:1–7 in appointed for the Second Sunday after Epiphany in Year A and on Tuesday in Holy Week.[3] The third song, 50:4–9, is heard notably on Palm Sunday and on Wednesday of Holy Week.[4] And the fourth, 52:13–53:12, is heard on Good Friday, so that it is particularly familiar.[5]

I have mentioned Handel's *Messiah* several times in the course of this work, as we have discussed one or another passage from Isaiah, but it is fair to say that the alto aria "He was despised," and the choruses "Surely He hath borne our griefs," "And with His stripes we are healed," and "All we like sheep have gone astray" form a backbone of recognition for English-speaking Christians whenever 53:1–6 is heard, in whatever translation. Indeed in the mind of Christians the association of the words of these passages with the mission and passion of Jesus is so tight that it takes an extra effort of the will for us to lay aside the association long enough to discern what Second Isaiah's hearers would have understanding in their circumstances. In my discussion of the third way to hear Isaiah in Chapter 1, I mentioned the difficulty I had in drafting a lecture to a joint audience of Christian clergy and Jewish rabbis on Isaiah 53. And the difficulties for Christians are increased because there is evidence that Jesus himself drew on these suffering servant texts for his own self-understanding (I shall return to this matter in Chapter 8). Nevertheless let us make the effort now to stand in the audience of Second Isaiah's hearers in the sixth century BCE.

The major question of course is: Who would those hearers have understood the servant to be? The matter is not at all clear. The first passage begins with the line,

"Here is my servant, whom I uphold" (42:1), and the fourth passage begins with the line, "See, my servant shall prosper" (52:13), but in neither passage is the servant identified.

Two things need to be said. The first is that there are several passages in chapters 40–55 outside the four Servant Songs in which there is an explicit identification of YAHWEH's servant—it is Israel. One notes, for example, 41:8, "But you, Israel, my servant, Jacob, whom I have chosen, the offspring of Abraham, my friend." Not only is Israel here identified as the servant, but the lines offer a parallel to "Israel," namely "Jacob," and this is the case in several of the other passages as well: in 44:1–2, 21; and 45:4. There are other passages in which Israel is identified as YAHWEH's servant but without a parallelism to "Jacob": 42:19 (compare 18); 43:10; 48:20; and by implication 44:26.

The second thing to say is that there is one spot in the four Servant Songs where the servant is identified. That is in 49:3, where the text reads, "And he said to me, 'You are my servant, Israel, in whom I will be glorified." This identification raised another problem. In v. 5a we read, "And now the LORD says, who formed me in the womb to be his servant, to bring Jacob back to him, and that Israel might be gathered to him," and in v. 6a, "He says, 'It is too light a thing that you should be my servant to raise up the tribes of Jacob and to restore the survivors of Israel.'" This passage suggests that the servant is to bring Israel back to God (and the "Israel" to be brought back to God is paralleled by "Jacob"). The question then is obvious: How can Israel bring back Israel? One can try to smoothe out the puzzle one way or another, but the wording is still awkward, and the conclusion of some scholars is that in 49:3 the word "Israel" is a very early interpolation in the text.

This still leaves us with the question of the identification of the servant in these four songs.

Of course many suggestions have been made through the centuries, particularly in the work of scholars of the past hundred years. Thus it has been suggested that the servant is a depiction of a saving remnant of Israel or Second Isaiah's depiction of himself. More to the point, it is clear both that the Servant is to some degree modeled after Jeremiah (see the discussion below on 53:2 and 7), and that there is a strong case to be made that the servant is intended to be a reminder of Moses.[6]

With regard to resemblances to Jeremiah and Moses several points need to be made:

* Deuteronomy 18:18 predicts that there will be a prophet "like Moses" in time to come, indeed perhaps a line of such prophets.[7]

* It is clear that Jeremiah in his day knew this passage and understood himself to be this prophet like Moses,[8] so the re-employment by Second Isaiah of this notion is cogent.

* Again and again in the tradition of Moses he is called "the servant of the LORD" (for example, Deuteronomy 34:5).

* Second Isaiah's notion, discussed in Chapter 4, of a new exodus out of Babylon, lends plausibility to the notion of a new Moses for that new exodus. I shall therefore adopt this notion of a new Moses in the discussion which follows.

In all this we must bear in mind that Second Isaiah was steadily and utterly in control of his rhetoric. That is to say, we cannot conclude that the prophet somehow should have done a better job in the way he expressed himself, to make clear precisely who the servant is here. Instead, our conclusion must be that if he did not leave a specific identification, he intended the identification to remain veiled. What remains unclear is whether he intended the hearers to work out the identification for themselves, or whether he intended to leave them as puzzled as we are, asking, as we do, "Whom is he talking about?"

But if the identification of the servant remains veiled, his task is altogether clear, and so it is to the job description that we turn. What is the servant to do? We look at the first song, in chapter 42:

(1)   Here is my servant, whom I uphold,
          my chosen, in whom my soul delights;
      I have put my spirit upon him;
          he will bring forth justice to the nations.

(2)   He will not cry or lift up his voice,
          or make it heard in the street;

(3)   a bruised reed he will not break,
          and a dimly burning wick he will not quench;
          he will faithfully bring forth justice.

(4)   He will not grow faint or be crushed
          until he has established justice in the earth;
          and the coastlands wait for his teaching.

The servant is the agent through whom YAHWEH accomplishes his justice among the nations (vv. 1, 4), but, strikingly, he does this gently. He is vulnerable. Indeed he is not even to raise his voice in the streets (vv. 2–3)! There is a nice wordplay in vv. 3–4 that the new Jewish translation (Tanakh) has caught: "He shall not break even a

bruised reed, or snuff out even a *dim* wick. He shall bring
forth the true way. He shall not grow *dim* or be *bruised*
till he has established the true way on earth." The Servant is strong but at the same time nonviolent.

These four verses are extended by 42:5–9 (see n. 1).
In vv. 6–7 YAHWEH addresses the servant, but this address
is framed by awesome self-descriptions of God the Creator (vv. 5, 8–9). If the servant is the agent through whom
God brings forth justice for the nations (v. 1), it is notably
to prisoners who sit in darkness (v. 7), so it is not justice
in general but quite specifically liberation that is meant.

In the second song, in chapter 49, the servant speaks
for himself: "The LORD called me before I was born" (v.
1). He announces himself to the nations of the world:
"Listen to me, O coastlands" (v. 1). He will be God's
weapon, though concealed: "He made my mouth like a
sharp sword, in the shadow of his hand he hid me" (v. 2).
Verse 3 drops a bombshell: "He said to me, 'You are my
servant, . . . in whom I will be glorified.'" It makes us wonder, "How's that again?"—God gains glory through the *servant?* In the call of the original Isaiah we had heard the
song of the seraphs around God's throne, "The whole
earth is full of his glory" (6:3). In the opening chapter of
Second Isaiah, he proclaims, "the glory of the LORD shall
be revealed" (40:5). How can God gain more glory? Especially when the servant expresses discouragement at his
lack of accomplishments: "But I said, 'I have labored in
vain, I have spent my strength for nothing and vanity,'" (v.
4). Yet he shall be a light to the nations, so that God's salvation may reach to the ends of the earth (v. 6). Listen to
YAHWEH's word to the servant.

> (7) Thus says the LORD,
>   the Redeemer of Israel and his Holy One,
>   To one deeply despised, abhorred by the nations,

> the slave of rulers,
> "Kings shall see and stand up,
>   princes, and they shall prostrate themselves,
> Because of the LORD, who is faithful,
>   the Holy One of Israel, who has chosen you."

The kings of the earth are accustomed to sitting and to giving orders, but at the servant's work even kings shall stand up and prostrate themselves! The whole world is turned upside down.

Again in the third servant song (50:4–9) we hear the servant speak for himself. He testifies that God has taught him (vv. 4–5), though in speaking out God's word he suffers persecution and insult. "I gave my back to those who struck me, and my cheeks to those who pulled out the beard; I did not hide my face from insult and spitting" (v. 6). Now there are many laments in the Old Testament in which the worshiper complains of ill treatment and persecution, particularly in the psalms. Look at Psalm 143:3–4, for example. But what is unprecedented here is that the servant accepts this treatment voluntarily. Through all this, however, he affirms that God is always close to help him and to vindicate him over against his enemies (vv. 7–9). We continue to wonder what this is all about.

The rhetoric comes to a climax in the fourth servant song (52:13–53:12). The last three verses of chapter 52 are a kind of preface.

> (13) See, my servant shall prosper;
>   he shall be exalted and lifted up,
>   and shall be very high.

> (14) Just as there were many who were astonished at him—
>   so marred was his appearance, beyond human

> semblance,
> and his form beyond that of mortals—

(15) so he shall startle many nations;
> kings shall shut their mouths because of him;
> for that which they had not been told them they
> shall see,
> > and that which they had not heard they shall
> > contemplate.

God's words in the very first verse come as a surprise; the servant shall be "exalted and lifted up," be "very high." We recall how the original Isaiah, in his call (6:1), understood God alone to be "high and lofty." Now, it seems, God's servant will share that privilege—an indication, like God's gaining glory through the servant (49:3), that an amazing reversal is underway.

Who are the "many" who are astonished at him (52:14)? Evidently "many nations" and "kings" (v. 15). They show they are astonished and startled by shutting their mouths. We heard back in chapter 40 that God makes the rulers of the earth as nothing (v. 23 there), and we heard in 49:7 that, because of what God has done in the servant, kings shall stand up and prostrate themselves. Here, the kings are silent. As we know, kings are always giving orders—go here; go there; off with his head! Kings simply do not shut their mouths, but these kings will. Why? Because "that which had not been told them they shall see." They shall see the exaltation of the servant, who has been so humiliated—"he was so inhumanly disfigured that he no longer looked like a man" (v. 14, *The New Jerusalem Bible*; he sounds like a leper). To the kings this makes no sense.

Now 53:1–6:

(1)   Who has believed what we have heard?
         And to whom has the arm of the LORD been
         revealed?

(2)   For he grew up before him like a young plant,
         and like a root out of dry ground;
      he had no form or majesty that we should look at him,
         nothing in his appearance that we should desire
         him.

(3)   He was despised and rejected by others;
         a man of suffering and acquainted with infirmity;
      and as one from whom others high their faces
         he was despised, and we held him of no account.

(4)   Surely he has borne our infirmities
         and carried our diseases;
      yet we accounted him stricken,
         struck down by God, and afflicted.

(5)   But he was wounded for our transgressions,
         crushed for our iniquities;
      upon him was the punishment that made us whole,
         and by his bruises we are healed.

(6)   All we like sheep have gone astray;
         we have all turned to our own way,
      and the LORD has laid on him
         the iniquity of us all.

Who are the "we" who speak in 53:1, 4–6? Evidently
those in Israel who do not yet understand. "Who has
believed" it? The implied answer is nobody. We do not for-
get that the servant is the secret weapon of YAHWEH
(49:2), so here he is still hidden. Nothing has been
revealed plainly yet.

Now the great story begins in all its mystery, with
words that echo from many directions in the ears of hearers. The servant grew up before God like a young plant,

and like a root out of dry ground (v. 2). This sounds like a line from Jeremiah (Jeremiah. 17:6) in which the desert shrub is used as a figure for someone who has lost his way altogether, who puts his trust in human beings instead of in God. Here is the paradox: the servant who is sponsored by God gives every evidence of being a good-for-nothing. Verse 2b picks up the theme of 52:14b. The servant has no beauty. In the Old Testament beauty implied blessing. Joseph had beauty (Genesis 30:6b); so did King David (1 Samuel 16:18). We know God was with these men. But this servant has no beauty, so how can we believe that God is with him? Indeed not only is the servant unattractive, he is positively rejected by everybody else. The phrasing in 53.3 suggests that people treat him like a leper (again, compare 52:14). He was "despised and rejected by others." This phrasing would remind hearers of Psalm 22:6b, "scorned by others, and despised by the people," the situation of someone in distress who calls to God for help. He is "a man of suffering and acquainted with infirmity." If the hearers had Moses in mind, one wonders, would they think of Exodus 4:6–8, the narrative in which Moses' hand became leprous and then was healed?

This possibility grows as we hear v. 4, "Surely he has borne our infirmities [singular in Hebrew, "infirmity"] and carried our diseases." A recent commentator has called attention to the narrative in Numbers 11–12.[9] In both chapters Moses is referred to as YAHWEH's servant (11:11; 12: 7, 8). In Numbers 11 it is emphasized several times that Moses must "carry" or "bear" the "burden" of the people (vv. 11, 12, 14, 17). Then in chapter 12 the authority of Moses is challenged by his sister Miriam and his brother Aaron. YAHWEH challenges the two: Miriam is afflicted with leprosy (v. 10), and Aaron confesses they have sinned (v. 11) and implores mercy for his sister (v.

12). Moses prays for her healing (v. 13), and the narrative implies that his prayer was answered. One suspects that this whole tissue of references forms a background for 53:4.

Now let us pause to ponder the close identification of sin and sickness in the Old Testament. In many of the psalms, for example, the speaker describes illness and then moves to the question, "What did I do wrong? why does God abandon me?" Psalm 88 is a good example. So as 53:4 moves to 53:5a, the hearers are led to the same thought. It is not just our *illness* that the servant has borne, but it is for our *wrongdoing* that he is wounded.

Not only does the servant take the punishment that the rest of Israel deserves, but his doing so heals them (v. 5b). The half-verse reads literally, "the discipline [or punishment] for our *shalom* [welfare, prosperity] is upon him, and by his wounds there is healing for us." Not only do the hearers go free when they deserve illness and punishment, but, when the servant takes on that illness and punishment, this act results in healing for them. It is not just that the hearers escape something negative—they gain something positive. They need what the servant can offer. If the figure of Moses is in the background, then we remind ourselves of the tradition that Moses suffered vicariously for his people. For example, in Deuteronomy 4:21 we hear Moses say, "The LORD was angry with me because of you, and he vowed that I should not cross the Jordan and that I should not enter the good land that the LORD your God is giving for your possession."

In v. 6 the hearers admit that they are like sheep without a shepherd. Hearers would recall Moses' words to YAH-WEH that he have a successor "so that the congregation of the LORD may not be like sheep without a shepherd" (Numbers 27:17). As the last half of the verse repeats, it is YAHWEH who has stricken the servant with the iniquity of all of us. The verse ends as it began.

> (7) He was oppressed, and he was afflicted,
>   yet he did not open his mouth;
>   like a lamb that is led to the slaughter,
>   and like a sheep that before its shearers is silent,
>   so he did not open his mouth.
>
> (8) By a perversion of justice he was taken away.
>   Who could have imagined his future?
>   For he was cut off from the land of the living,
>   stricken for the transgression of my people.
>
> (9) They made his grave with the wicked
>   and his tomb with the rich,
>   although he had done no violence;
>   and there was no deceit in his mouth.

Verses 7 and 8 offer a remarkable series of passive verbs: "he was oppressed," "he was afflicted," "he was taken away," "he was cut off." Actions are done *to* the servant, but the focus is steadily on the servant himself. Verse 7 repeats the theme of v. 4 and then reaches back to 42:2 in the first servant song. The servant will not raise his voice. Then, in a fresh image strongly reminiscent of Jeremiah's complaints to God (Jeremiah 11:19), the servant is compared to a sheep led to the slaughter. Jeremiah certainly suffered as a prophet, but this is a new note. We have heard of the servant's wounds and pains, but the mention of slaughter is ominous. Furthermore, "they made his grave with the wicked." This again seems to suggest Moses, who did not live to dwell in the promised land, but whose grave was in Moab. Moses is buried opposite Beth-peor (Deuteronomy 34:6). Hos. 9:10 associates wickedness with "Peor," a name in turn associated with pagan worship (Numbers 25:1–13, compare Psalm106:28). Moses bore the sin of his people and was buried with the wicked. That is evidently the template for these verses.

> (10) Yet it was the will of the Lord to crush him
>   with pain.
> When you make his life an offering for sin,
>   he shall see his offspring, and shall prolong
>   his days;
> through him the will of the Lord shall prosper.

This verse begins the closing portion of the passage. The first line underlines God's purpose in the whole enterprise. If any bystanders at this drama are loyal to YAHWEH, it would be natural, for them to think that YAHWEH's servant being led away suggests that the deity is somehow absentminded or weak. But no, v. 10 affirms twice that all of this is YAHWEH's will. It is YAHWEH's will that his servant be crushed. There is now a great reversal. The servant shall see his offspring! YAHWEH's servant shall prosper, and he shall prosper by YAHWEH's will. How this great reversal comes about is left unstated, but through it all YAHWEH is very much in charge. YAHWEH does not leave the servant in a forgotten grave (compare Deuteronomy 34:6) but vindicates him before the world. Verses 11b–12 recapitulate the drama, just to make sure we have heard it rightly: "He bore the sin of many, and made intercession for the transgressors."

Those who have been guilty (53:5) are now pronounced innocent. All of this, as I have said, turns everything that Israel had held true and dear upside down. Listen to the old law: "Keep far from a false charge, and do not kill the innocent and those in the right, for I will not acquit the guilty" (Exodus 23:7). What God had forbidden Israelites to do, *God* now does, allowing an innocent servant to suffer and through this even treating the guilty as innocent. All Israel's familiar landmarks have fallen.

What a story! If it were not so familiar it would hit us with the same thunderclap with which it must have hit Second Isaiah's first hearers. The very servant of God suffers, and suffers undeservedly for the rest of the people.

Let us ponder the matter of suffering for a moment. Basically there were two related explanations among the Israelites as to why people suffer. The first was that suffering is punitive: if you suffered, it was because you deserved to. We saw this in the identification of sickness with sin in vv. 4–5. Of course this notion was easier to sustain when people believed in the solidarity of family and clan. When notions of individuality were not strongly developed, and when families and clans were tightknit, then if an individual's suffering and sin did not always match up, one assumed that the sins of the *parents* were visited upon the children (compare Exodus 20:5).

The second, related notion was that suffering is pedagogic—it teaches a lesson. There is a lot of this in the book of Proverbs. "The rod and reproof give wisdom," (Proverbs 29:15). We got a hint of this in Chapter 4 when we looked at Isaiah 40:2. Jerusalem "has received from the LORD's hand *double* for all her sins"—twice as much as she deserves.

Valid though these explanations are, they hardly lift the spirit. In any event, various authorities came along to challenge the notion of family and clan solidarity while the people were dislocated by exile in Babylon. Ezekiel announced the annulment of the old proverb, "The parents have eaten sour grapes, and the children's teeth are set on edge." No, instead "it is only the person who sins that shall die" (Ezekiel 18:2, 4; compare Jeremiah 31:29–30).

That God does not employ double-entry bookkeeping with sin and suffering is fresh news from Second Isaiah. Suffering is not always simply punitive or pedagogic but has a positive part to play in God's new work as well. God's servant is to live out a life of humiliation and suffering, not for any sins he has committed in the past, but for the future rescue of others. The servant is called to innocent suffering, and when he accepts his calling and is faithful to that calling in the totality of his life, then God will highly exalt him. Second Isaiah is mute about the identity of this figure who so repeatedly reminds his hearers of Moses and Jeremiah, but his very muteness cries out to Israel, "Ponder the task!"

We must save an exploration of how later Jews and Christians took the story of the servant until the last two chapters of this book. What matters for us at this point is that within the Old Testament itself there is virtually no subsequent trace of the influence of the story. The theme was not taken up, or tried, or explored.[10] The hearers of Second Isaiah's time evidently were not so sure it was good news. They were content, so far as our record goes, to stay with the prophet's overtly good news, that God is active and that they were going home (see Chapters 4 and 5).

GOD CALLS ISRAEL TO ACT

Let us turn now to chapters 56–66 of the book of Isaiah. If, as we saw at the beginning of Chapter 4, Isaiah 40–55 offers sixteen chapters of awesome news about what God is going to do, chapters 56–66 are much more mixed. It is true, three of these chapters, chapters 60–62, form a joyful centerpiece, offering much the same vistas as we glimpsed in chapters 40–55, but the material before and after these chapters reflects in many ways a troubled people. We need to orient ourselves, therefore, to the likely historical context for this section of the book.

Even though scholars differ on the question, I have my own strong reasons to believe that these eleven chapters of Isaiah are likewise the work of Second Isaiah. Beyond a few supplementary additions, they are proclaimed in a new burst of prophecy some twenty-five years after the material in chapters 40–55 which we have already compassed.[11] At least for ease of presentation I shall take this tack here.

The locale is no longer Babylon but Jerusalem. Cyrus conquered Babylon in 538 BCE and allowed many of the Jewish exiles, including, evidently, Second Isaiah himself, to return to Jerusalem. They found Jerusalem sadly depleted of resources and population. Those who returned made a start in rebuilding the temple, but work lapsed. Then, a generation later, Cyrus's successor Darius sent a fresh contingent of Jews back to Jerusalem, and a fresh start was made on the temple. In 516 it was finally completed.

Some of these passages offer fretful invective against a coterie of corrupt and insensitive religious leaders, for example, 56:9–12. Evidently it was not easy for the prophet to continue to maintain his splendid vision in the midst of the daily struggles undertaken by those who returned.

Let us begin at the beginning, with 56:1–8.[12] God speaks. Verse 1 reads, "Thus says the LORD: Maintain justice, and do what is right, for soon my salvation will come, and my deliverance be revealed." The word "soon" strikes us as odd, as if people are getting restless for the glorious future they had been promised, as if they were being told to hang on just a little longer. If we have been paying careful attention to chapters 40–55, the injunction to "maintain justice, and do what is right" is also curious. In those earlier chapters we heard nothing about people's right conduct, only about the glories of God's conduct. Now the prophet urges obedience to God's law. "Happy is the mortal . . . who keeps the sabbath" (56:2) is likewise striking. The previous chapters have said nothing about the sabbath. Apparently in these decades the Jewish sabbath was taking on fresh significance as one of the most important ways to maintain the identity of a people who no longer could depend on borders and political leadership to define themselves.

The focus of the passage turns out to be the question of who is allowed into worship in the newly rebuilt temple. Verse 7 twice has the phrase "house of prayer." God wants worship to be open to foreigners (that is, Jewish converts) and eunuchs. The prophet rejects the validity of old laws like those in Deuteronomy 23:1–2, in order deliberately to include within the worshiping community those whom the more narrow-minded authorities would exclude.

In the last section of chapter 57, a passage that turns up in our lectionaries, one hears reassurance.[13]

> (15) For thus says the high and lofty one
>   who inhabits eternity, whose name is Holy:
>   I dwell in the high and holy place,
>   and also with those who are contrite and
>   humble in spirit,
>   to revive the spirit of the humble,
>   and to revive the heart of the contrite.

This is the same description of God as the high, lofty, holy one that we found in 6:1–3 (see Chapter 2), but the stress here is on God's reviving the spirit of the humble and contrite. It is clear that the prophet is speaking to a demoralized people. In 57:17 it is said that even though God had been angry—as when the people were sent into exile—that anger will not last. "Peace, peace, to the far and near, says the LORD" (v. 19).

Several sequences of chapter 58 are chosen for the lectionaries, notably the opening verses in association with Ash Wednesday.[14] It is a chapter concerned with fasting. The people ask God, "Why do we fast, but you do not see? Why humble ourselves, but you do not notice?" God answers, "Look, you serve your own interest on your fast day, and oppress all your workers" (v. 3). Fasting unaccompanied by justice, mercy, and sharing is empty (vv. 6–7). The verses of this chapter again give the impression of a society that is both in need and riven by conflict (vv. 3b–4, 12). Once again, sabbath observance, about which we heard in 56:2, 6, is mentioned (vv. 13–14).

A large section of chapter 59 is heard in the Episcopal lectionary.[15] Verses 1–4 depict a violent and litigious community. The prophet speaks in v. 1: "See, the LORD's hand is not too short to save, nor his ear too dull to hear." It sounds as though the people are tempted to wonder whether God is not too weak to do what has been promised! The prophet insists, rather, that it is the misdeeds of the people that keep salvation at bay (vv. 2–4). Verses 5–8 offer a metaphorical description of these misdeeds, but they are evidently too vivid to be included in any lectionary reading. Instead of offering bread to the hungry (which we heard about in 58:7a), they hatch snakes' eggs (59:5), and instead of offering clothes to the naked (which we heard about in 58:7b), they weave a spider's web (59:5–6). The people stumble along (vv. 9–15), so that finally God himself must intervene like a warrior (vv. 16–19; compare 42:13, discussed in Chapter 4).

Then suddenly, in chapter 60, there is light. The beginning of this chapter is the lection every year for the First Sunday after the Epiphany.[16]

(1)   Arise, shine; for your light has come,
         and the glory of the LORD has risen upon you.

(2)   For darkness shall cover the earth,
         and thick darkness the peoples;
      but the LORD will arise upon you,
         and his glory will appear over you.

(3)   Nations shall come to your light,
         and kings to the brightness of your dawn.

The entire chapter is an address to Jerusalem, and since cities are feminine in Hebrew, the address in this whole chapter is in the feminine singular. The acoustic effect in the original language is remarkable. The vulnerable female is honored by nations and kings. God's light will shine on Jerusalem. Not only will the city's sons and daughters stream in (v. 4), but the riches of the whole world as well (vv. 5–6).

Chapters 61 and 62 form overlapping sequences of lessons that are heard on various occasions, especially during the Advent, Christmas, and Epiphany seasons.[17] Here are the first four verses of chapter 61:

(1)   The spirit of the Lord GOD is upon me,
         because the LORD has anointed me;
      he has sent me to bring good news to the oppressed,
         to bind up the brokenhearted,
      to proclaim liberty to the captives,
         and release to the prisoners;

(2)   to proclaim the year of the LORD's favor,
         and the day of vengeance of our God;
      to comfort all who mourn;

(3)   to provide for those who mourn in Zion—
         to give them a garland instead of ashes,
      the oil of gladness instead of mourning,
         the mantle of praise instead of a faint spirit.

> They will be called oaks of righteousness,
> the planting of the LORD, to display his glory.

(4) They shall build up the ancient ruins,
> they shall raise up the former devastations;
> they shall repair the ruined cities,
> the devastations of many generations.

At the beginning of Chapter 4 we glimpsed just a shadow of Second Isaiah's own person in the expression "I said" (40:6). Here we glimpse just a shadow of the prophet's own person in the use of "me" and "I" in vv. 1 and 10. At the end of Chapter 1, I cited Calvin's use of 61:1 to refer both to the prophet and to Jesus Christ. Christians are so accustomed to hearing the passage that they need to be reminded that it was a *prophet* whom God has anointed, but to the prophet's original hearers this would have been shocking. Recall the discussion in Chapter 4 on the designation "anointed." Traditionally it referred to the Davidic king, but in 45:1 God metaphorically anointed a king who was not in the line of David, namely Cyrus, the Persian king. Now, it seems, we have another figure metaphorically anointed, not a king but the prophet himself. The prophet is here underlining the legitimacy of his words.

What is his calling to be? To announce good news! In chapters 40–55 we heard of good news ("good tidings" in 40:9; 41:27; "good news" in 52:7), but that news was destined for Zion, for Jerusalem. Now it is good news to the oppressed, the brokenhearted, the captives, the prisoners, the mourners—to all the faceless, forgotten ones, who have lost hope, if indeed they ever had any. We recall the task of the servant to bring out from prison those who sit in darkness, 42:7. It is to them that God directs his prophetic word. It is they who are at the center of God's action. Look at that action: binding up, proclaiming liberty,

comforting. It is the afflicted, not the pillars of society, not
"Israel's sentinels," not the ignorant "shepherds"
(56:10–11), who are destined to "build up the ancient
ruins" (61:4). The reversal continues: other nations shall
be servants to you (v. 5). If you suffered double for all your
sins (40:2), now you shall enjoy a double portion (v. 7).
No wonder the prophet is ecstatic (vv. 10–11)!

The first-person references continue in 62:1: "For Zion's
sake I will not keep silent, and for Jerusalem's sake I will
not rest, until her vindication shines out like the dawn, and
her salvation like a burning torch." Apparently it is still the
prophet who speaks. Jerusalem will gain fresh brilliance. Her
new names in the world will be (v. 4), Hephzibah ("my
delight is in her") and Beulah ("married")—married
metaphorically to YAHWEH. No longer shall people be
haunted by the old negative names announced by Hosea or
Jeremiah, names signaling YAHWEH's rejection of his consort people (see Hosea1:8–9; 2:2; Jeremiah 30:17). Now
God will embark upon a new, intimate beginning with them.

In 62:6–12 the discourse continues. "Upon your
walls, O Jerusalem, I have posted sentinels; all day and
all night they shall never be silent" (v. 6). The function of
the watchmen is to remind YAHWEH of his promise to
establish Jerusalem as the prosperous center of all the
world (vv. 7–9). The chapter ends (v. 12) with reinforce-
ments of the name change of which we heard in v. 4.

Most of chapters 63–64 are taken up with a long
lament psalm (63:7–64:12). It is striking how the inclu-
sions and omissions in the lectionaries of various verses
of this sequence, and the order in which the stanzas are
heard by Christians, all combine to give an impression
rather different than the original sequence.[18] The opening verses, 63:7–9, stress YAHWEH's steady presence and
favor to Israel, but in vv. 10–15, not used in the

lectionaries, we hear of the people's ungracious rebellion against YAHWEH (v. 10) and of their pathetic question about where YAHWEH's zeal on their behalf has gone. Their questions continue in 63:16–19 with the implication that if the people stray, it is God's fault (v. 17a). Listen now to the first two verses of chapter 64.

> (1) O that you would tear open the heavens and come
>   down,
>   so that the mountains would quake at your
>   presence—
>   as when fire kindles brushwood
>   and the fire causes water to boil—
>   to make your name known to your adversaries,
>   so that the nations might tremble at your presence!

We have traveled a long way from 2:10–17, words of the original Isaiah two centuries before. The people admit their guilt in 64:5–6, but beg God to return once more in (vv. 8–9).

God's reassuring answer comes in the first part of chapter 65.[19] Verse 1 reads:

> (1) I was ready to be sought out by those who did not ask,
>   to be found by those who did not seek me.
>   I said, "Here I am, here I am,"
>   to a nation that did not call on my name.

The last nine verses of chapter 65 are heard in several different contexts in our lectionaries.[20] In a kind of climax God speaks.

> (17) For I am about to create new heavens
>   and a new earth;
>   the former things shall not be remembered
>   or come to mind.

. . . .

> (19) I will rejoice in Jerusalem,
>   and delight in my people;
>   no more shall the sound of weeping be heard in it,
>   or the cry of distress.

These are the themes we have already heard in chapter 40–55, but now the details move well beyond the descriptions of the desert turned to garden land. Now there will be no more infant mortality (v. 20), no more expropriation of buildings and vineyards in which people have invested so much work (vv. 21–22), and by implication, no more military conquest. God will listen to people's prayers (v. 24), and in all creation, violence will cease and become a thing of the past—even the violence of wild animals (v. 25). We note here that 65:25 is a short form of 11:6–9. It is altogether possible then, as I suggested in Chapter 3, that those verses early in the book of Isaiah are an expansion inserted by our sixth century prophet onto the description of the future righteous king.

Chapter 66 appears to be made up of several miscellaneous utterances. Three of them figure in our lectionaries. The first is vv. 1–2, curiously the Old Testament reading in the Lutheran lectionary for the Festival of St. Matthias.[21] I say "curiously" because the passage is the beginning of a divine word, spoken through the prophet, that questions the whole notion of rebuilding the temple in Jerusalem. It is not clear how this passage is associated with Matthias (Acts 1:15–26) unless the general approbation of the "humble and contrite in spirit" would fit him. The second passage begins in v. 10.[22] The verses up through v. 14 describe a new Jerusalem in glowing terms, but vv. 15–16 add the note that Yahweh will come with fire to execute judgment. And the third is vv. 18–21,[23] a vision of God gathering all nations to Jerusalem.

We have now completed our survey of Isaiah 35 and 40–66, all chapters that, by the understanding of this work, are from the hand of Second Isaiah. At the beginning of Chapter 4, when I introduced Second Isaiah, I set forth Hugh Williamson's proposal that Second Isaiah had a major share in rearranging the material of the first Isaiah. It is relevant now to add one more chapter to the list of rearranged material, chapter 12. This chapter, in Williamson's analysis, was drafted by Second Isaiah to close off the primary collection of material from the original Isaiah (chapters 1–11). I cite it here because it figures as a response (that is, as a substitution for the normal Psalm reading), in both Advent and in the Easter Vigil.[24] Its note is *joy* (v. 6).

It remains, finally, to mention a few miscellaneous passages that appear to have been added after the composition of chapters 56–66 (that is, after 515 BCE). One is 4:2–6, the fourth reading at the Great Vigil of Easter in the Episcopal lectionary.[25] It speaks (v. 5) of God's presence in Jerusalem in ways like the desert wanderings. Another is 25:1–10, all or part of which is used at several points in the Church year.[26] Verses 1–5 are a kind of psalm of thanksgiving (and it may be noted that vv. 4-5 are similar to 4:5–6), while vv. 6–10 depict a feast "on this mountain" (Zion, in Jerusalem, v. 6) at which God will "wipe away the tears from all faces" (v. 8). Still another is various portions of chapter 26, also used at several points in the Church year.[27] Verses 1–6 are a hymn of praise over Jerusalem, and vv. 7–19 are a kind of apocalyptic psalm that affirms, in the end time, a resurrection for the righteous and oblivion for unjust rulers.

In the ways I have described, then, with the participation of who-knows-how-many folk who spoke for God, the whole book of Isaiah took final written shape, most likely by the end of the fifth century BCE. In Chapter 1 of this work I described a second way of hearing the texts of Isaiah, namely that they were speaking to their own generation, and in Chapters 2 through 6 we have worked through this second way by attempting to hear the texts in their historical contexts. Now we must move to the third way, seeing how the faith communities that inherited Isaiah heard the texts. This will be our task in Chapters 7 and 8.

NOTES

1. There has been disagreement among scholars as to extent of the first two of the Songs. With regard to the sequence in chapter 42 opinion varies widely. To take only two representative views, James Muilenburg understood 42:1–4 to close the section he calls "The Trial of the Nations" (41:1–42:4), and 42:5–9 to introduce the section he calls "The New Event of the Divine Intervention" (42:5–17); see *The Interpreter's Bible*, 5 (New York/Nashville: Abingdon, 1956).

2. Verses 1–9 of chapter 42 are set forth for the Sunday between January 7 and 13 in the Episcopal lectionary (called "the First Sunday after the Epiphany") for every year, and in the Revised Common Lectionary (called "the Baptism of the Lord") for Year A only. For those other than Roman Catholics, Epiphany is always observed on January 6 and the Baptism of the Lord is observed on the Sunday between January 7 and 13. For Roman Catholics the two are usually observed separately, Epiphany on the Sunday between January 2 and 8 and the Baptism of the Lord on the Sunday between January 9 and 13, but if in a given year the only Sunday falls on January 7 or 8, Epiphany takes precedence. In the lectionaries of all communities this lection is used for every observance of the Baptism of the Lord, though the Lutherans read only vv. 1–7, and the Roman Catholics read only vv. 1–4 and 6–7. The passage is also set forth in all the lectionaries for Monday in Holy Week, though the Roman Catholic lectionary uses only vv. 1–7; the other lections use all nine verses. Verses 1–7 are also chosen in the Episcopal lectionary for the liturgy for social justice, and vv. 1–3 are an alternative reading for Confirmation in the Roman Catholic lectionary. It is also to be noted that vv. 5–12 are the Old Testament lesson in the Episcopal and Lutheran lectionaries for the feast of St. Barnabas, June 11.

3. Verses 1–7 of chapter 49 are appointed for the Sunday between January 14 and 20 in Year A in the Revised Common Lectionary and

the Episcopal lectionary. On the same Sunday the Roman Catholic lectionary appoints vv. 3 and 5–6. For Tuesday of Holy Week the Revised Common Lectionary and the Episcopal lectionary use vv. 1–6. Verses 1–6 are also used in the Roman Catholic lectionary for the Mass during the day at the feast of John the Baptist, June 24, and in the Episcopal lectionary for the second set of readings for the common of a missionary. It is also to be noted that vv. 5–13 are chosen in the Episcopal lectionary for the second set of readings for the mission of the Church.

4. Verses 4–9a of chapter 50 are set forth for the Liturgy of the Passion (on Palm Sunday) in the Revised Common Lectionary for the Old Testament reading every year, and on the same occasion the Roman Catholic lectionary uses vv. 4–7. Verses 4–9a are used in the Lutheran lectionary for Palm Sunday only in Year A. The passage is not used on Palm Sunday in the Episcopal lectionary. Verses 4–9a are used in all the lectionaries every year for Wednesday of Holy Week. The same passage is also read on the Sunday between September 11 and 17 in Year B in the Roman Catholic, Episcopal, and Lutheran lectionaries (but not on that Sunday in the Revised Common Lectionary). It is also an alternative reading for the Votive Mass for the Holy Cross in the Roman Catholic lectionary.

5. The passage is appointed in all the lectionaries for the Old Testament lesson on Good Friday, and it is also an alternative Old Testament reading every year for the Liturgy of the Word on Palm Sunday in the Episcopal lectionary. For the Sunday between October 16 and 22 in Year B in the Episcopal and Lutheran lectionaries 53:4–12 is appointed, and in the Roman Catholic lectionary 53:10–11 is appointed. The Revised Common Lectionary does not use any of the passage on that occasion. The reading is also appointed on an occasion of the Holy Cross in the Episcopal lectionary and as an alternative reading for the Votive Mass on the Holy Cross in the Roman Catholic lectionary. Verses 1–5 and 10–11 of chapter 53 are appointed as an alternative reading for the Mass for the sick in the Roman Catholic lectionary.

6. There is an enormous literature on the question. See Horacio Simian-Yofre, *ā<u>b</u>a<u>d</u>*, etc.," in G. Johannes Botterweck et al.; *Theological Dictionary of the Old Testament* 10 (Grand Rapids: Eerdmans, 1999), 376–78, literature note. For a judicious assessment of various suggestions of the identity of the Servant see Gerhard von Rad, *The Theology of Israel's Prophetic Traditions, Vol. 2 Old Testament Theology;* (New York: Harper & Row, 1965), 250–62. For a full survey of resemblances to Jeremiah see Benjamin D. Sommer, *A Prophet Reads Scripture, Allusion in Isaiah 40–66* (Stanford: Stanford University

Press, 1998), 64–66. For a recent discussion of the relation between Moses and the Servant see Ronald E. Clements, "Isaiah 53 and the Restoration of Israel," in William H. Bellinger, Jr., and William R. Farmer (eds.), *Jesus and the Suffering Servant and the Suffering Servant, Isaiah 53 and Christian Origins* (Harrisburg, PA: Trinity, 1998), 47–54. For a vigorous defense of the identification see Baltzer, *Deutero-Isaiah*, 20–22.

7. On a succession of such prophets see von Rad, op. cit., 261, n. 44.

8. William L. Holladay, "The Background of Jeremiah's Self-Understanding: Moses, Samuel, and Psalm 22," *Journal of Biblical Literature* 83 (1964) 153–65; "Jeremiah and Moses: Further Observations," *Journal of Biblical Literature* 85 (1966) 17–27; von Rad, op. cit., 261.

9. Baltzer, *Deutero-Isaiah*, 408.

10. There appears to be one exception. The description in Daniel 11.33, "The wise among the people shall give understanding to many," is derived from Isaiah 52:13 and 53:11, since "shall prosper" in 52:13 is related to the Hebrew word translated "wise" in Daniel 11:33. The background of the book of Daniel is Jewish resistance to the hated Hellenistic king Antiochus about 165 BCE, so the author is using the description of the servant to describe those who are prudent in his own day. See H. Louis Ginsberg, "The Old Interpretation of the Suffering Servant," *Vetus Testamentum* 3 (1953): 400–404; John J. Collins, *Daniel* (Hermeneia; Minneapolis: Fortress, 1993), 385.

11. William L. Holladay, "Was Trito-Isaiah Deutero-Isaiah After All?" *Writing and Reading the Scroll of Isaiah* (in Craig C. Broyles and Craig A. Evans; Supplements to Vetus Testamentum 70; Leiden: Brill, 1997), 193–218.

12. Three lectionaries use portions of this passage for the Sunday between August 14 and 20 in Year A. The Lutheran lectionary uses vv. 1, 6–8, the Roman Catholic lectionary uses vv. 1, 6–7, and the Episcopalian lectionary uses vv. 1–5, 6–7. Beyond that Sunday vv. 1–3, 6–8 are read in the Roman Catholic weekday lectionary for Friday of the Third Week of Advent, and vv. 1, 6–7 compose an alternative reading in the Roman Catholic lectionary for two occasions—for the common of the dedication of a church and for the Mass for the spread of the gospel.

13. Verses 14b–21 are the Old Testament lesson in the Episcopal lectionary for the Sunday between July 17 and 23 in Year B. Verses 15–19 compose an alternative reading in the Roman Catholic lectionary for two occasions—for the Mass for Independence Day in the United States (July 4), and for a Mass for peace and justice.

14. In the Revised Common Lectionary and in the Lutheran lectionary vv. 1–12 are an alternative reading for Ash Wednesday; in the Roman Catholic daily lectionary vv. 1–9 are heard on the Friday after Ash Wednesday, and vv. 9–14 on the Saturday after Ash Wednesday. For the Fifth Sunday after Epiphany (the Sunday between February 4 and 10) in Year A vv. 1–9a (with the optional addition of 9b–12) are chosen in the Revised Common Lectionary and vv. 7–10 in the Roman Catholic Lectionary. Verses 9b–14 are chosen in the Lutheran lectionary for the Sunday between August 21 and 27 in Year C. Verses 6–11 also serve as an alternative reading in the Roman Catholic lectionary on two occasions—for the common of holy men and women, especially those who work for the disadvantaged, and for the Mass for those suffering from famine or hunger.

15. Verses 9–19, optionally prefixed by vv. 1–4, are appointed for the Sunday between October 23 and 29 in Year B.

16. All the lectionaries use vv. 1–6, and the Episcopal lectionary adds v. 9. It is also to be noted that vv. 1-6 is an alternative reading for the Roman Catholic Mass for the spread of the gospel, and that portions of the chapter form what the Episcopal lectionary calls "Canticle 11," "The Third Song of Isaiah, *Surge, illuminare*," that is, vv. 1–3, 11a, 14c, 18–19, an alternative canticle for Morning Prayer.

17. Portions of chapter 61 are heard on the Third Sunday of Advent in Year B. For that Sunday vv. 1–4 and 8–11 are chosen in the Revised Common Lectionary, vv. 1–2 and 10–11 in the Roman Catholic lectionary; it is not, however, the reading on that occasion in the Episcopal lectionary. Verses 1–9 are an alternative reading for confirmation—all nine verses for Episcopalians, vv. 1–3, 6, 8–9 for Roman Catholics. Verses 1–3 are set for various occasions connected with ordination in the Roman Catholic and Episcopal lectionaries. In the Roman Catholic lectionary, they are used for holy orders for bishops and priests, for the election of a pope or bishop, and (as an alternative reading outside the Easter season) for the Common of Pastors; in the Episcopal lectionary, they are used for the occasion of the Holy Spirit. Verses 7–11 are the reading for the Festival of Mary, Mother of Our Lord (August 15) in the Lutheran lectionary; vv. 10–11 are likewise the reading for the feast of St. Mary the Virgin (August 15) in the Episcopal lectionary, and though this date is the solemnity of the Assumption of the Virgin Mary for Roman Catholics, Isaiah 61 is not used by them on this occasion. Verses 9–11 *are* used by Roman Catholics, however, as an alternative reading for the Common of the Blessed Virgin Mary (for example, for Saturday celebrations of Mary), for votive Masses for the Blessed Virgin Mary, and for the Mass for

the Consecration of Virgins and Religious Profession. Verses 10–11 of chapter 61 are linked to 62:1–3 in lectionary readings for the First Sunday after Christmas: for every year in the Episcopal lectionary, and for that Sunday in Year B in the Revised Common Lectionary and in the Lutheran lectionary. These five verses are not in the Roman Catholic lectionary, but 61:10–62:5 is the canticle in the Roman Catholic Liturgy of the Hours for morning prayer for Wednesday of Week IV. Verses 1–5 of chapter 62 are used in the Roman Catholic lectionary for the Mass of the Christmas Vigil and in other lectionaries for the Sunday between January 14 and 20 in Year C. Verses 6–12 of chapter 62 are offered in the Revised Common Lectionary as the first set of alternative lections for Christmas Eve or Christmas Day, and in the Lutheran lectionary as the second set of lections for the service for Dawn on Christmas Day. Verses 6–7 and 10–12 are appointed in the Episcopal lectionary for the second service for Christmas Day, and vv. 11–12 are appointed in the Roman Catholic lectionary for the Mass at Dawn on Christmas Day.

18. The first three verses, 63:7–9, are chosen in the Revised Common Lectionary, and thus in the Lutheran lectionary, for the First Sunday after Christmas in Year A. The passage is also an alternative reading for a Mass in Thanksgiving in the Roman Catholic lectionary. It does not occur in the Episcopal lectionary. Portions of 63:16–64:9 are chosen in the lectionaries for the First Sunday of Advent in Year B: the Roman Catholic lectionary uses 63:16–17, 19; 64:2–7, but without a conjunction at the beginning, simply "You, Lord, are our father." The Revised Common Lectionary and therefore the Lutheran lectionary use 64:1–9, and the Episcopal lectionary uses 64:1–9a.

19. The first nine verses of chapter 65 are an alternative reading in the Revised Standard Lectionary, and therefore the Lutheran lectonary, for the Sunday between June 19 and 25 in Year C. They do not appear in the Roman Catholic or Episcopal lectionaries.

20. Verses 17–25 of the chapter are found in the Episcopal lectionary for the Third Sunday in Advent in Year B. It is an alternative reading in the Revised Common Lectionary (and therefore for the Lutheran lectionary) for Easter in Year C, and it is found in the Revised Common Lectionary (and therefore for the Lutheran lectionary) for the Sunday between November 13 and 19 in Year C. Verses 17–21 are assigned in the Roman Catholic weekend lectionary for the Monday of the Fourth Week in Lent.

21. This feast has traditionally been celebrated on February 24 in the

Western Church. Though this day likewise marks the feast in the Episcopal church, the lectionary of the latter does not use 66:1–2 here. The feast has been shifted to May 14 in the Roman Catholic calendar. The passage is not used in that lectionary either.

22. It is for the Sunday between July 3 and 9 in Year C. The Episcopal lectionary uses vv. 10–16; vv. 10–14 are used in the Roman Catholic and Lutheran lectionaries. Verses 10–14 are also chosen in the Roman Catholic lectionary for the feasts of Our Lady of Lourdes, February 11, and of St. Theresa of the Child Jesus (the "Little Flower of Jesus"), October 1. The passage is also the canticle in the Liturgy of the Hours for morning prayer for Thursday of Week IV.

23. This passage is found in the Roman Catholic lectionary for the Sunday between August 21 and 27 in Year C.

24. Verses 2–6 serve as the response after the reading of Isaiah 55:1–11 in the Easter Vigil in the Revised Common Lectionary and in the Roman Catholic lectionary, and an alternative response at that point in the vigil in the Episcopal lectionary. They likewise serve as the response on the Third Sunday of Advent in Year C in the Revised Common Lectionary and the Roman Catholic lectionary, and an alternative response on that Sunday in the Episcopal lectionary. The whole chapter serves as a response on the Sunday between November 13 and 19 in Year C in the Revised Common Lectionary. One may note that in the Liturgy of the Hours for Roman Catholics the whole chapter is the canticle for Moning Prayer for Thursday in Week II, and that vv. 2–6 make up "Canticle 9, the First Song of Isaiah, *Ecce Deus*," an alternative canticle for Morning Prayer in the Episcopal Book of Common Prayer.

25. It is also the first reading for Monday of the first week of Advent in Year A in the Roman Catholic weekday lectionary.

26. Verses 1–9 are the reading for the Sunday between October 9 and 15 in Year A in the Episcopal and Lutheran lectionaries. Verses 6–10 are chosen for that occasion in the Roman Catholic lectionary, and likewise for the Wednesday of the first week of Advent in the Roman Catholic weekday lectionary. Verses 6–10 serve as a reading in the Revised Common Lectionary for Easter evening, as an alternative reading for Easter in Year B, and as a reading for All Saints (November 1) in Year B. The Episcopal lectionary likewise lists these verses as an alternative reading for Easter in Year B. The passage also figures in occasional liturgies: vv. 6–10 at the Roman Catholic Mass for a Happy Death; vv. 6–9 as an alternative reading in the Episcopal liturgy for the departed; vv. 6a, 7–9 as an alternative reading for

the Roman Catholic Mass for All Souls (November 2) and for the burial of a child.

27. Verses 2–9 and 19 are an alternative reading in the Episcopal lectionary for the Second Sunday of Easter in Year B. In the Roman Catholic weekday lectionary vv. 1–6 are the reading for Thursday of the first week of Advent, and vv. 7–9, 12, 16–19 are the reading for the Thursday between July 14 and 20 in Year II. Verses 1–8 are the Old Testament lesson in the Episcopal lectionary on the occasion of a liturgy for the nation.

Chapter 7

Jews Hear Isaiah
Through the Centuries

FOR MANY CHRISTIAN READERS this chapter will seem like an interruption to the smooth sweep from passages in the book of Isaiah itself, through their citations in the New Testament, and on through Christian proclamation. But it is not an interruption at all, because it offers an alternate stream of tradition out of the book of Isaiah into the present time. As such it is a prime example of the third way of hearing the texts of Isaiah which I set forth in Chapter 1, namely that there can be multiple "real time" meanings to the texts.

We turn then to the tradition of Jewish interpretation of Isaiah. Jewish communities have drawn on the book of Isaiah ever since it took shape. They did so steadily for centuries before the Christian movement emerged and have continued to do so steadily down to the present day.

If the Christian stream of tradition is intricate for non-Christians, the Jewish stream is intricate for Christians. We Christians need at least an outline of the ways Jews have used Isaiah if only to gain a better perspective on our own interpretive moves.

Indeed, beyond a knowledge of the Jewish traditional use of Scripture, we need a clearer grasp of the history of the Jewish people in the last two millennia. Most of our impressions about Jews in ancient times are gained from the Bible. All too often there is a yawning gap in our awareness, a gap of the nineteen centuries between the Jews who are depicted in the book of Acts and the Jews who today are our next-door neighbors. For purposes of this chapter, we will content ourselves with the following seven historical landmarks:

1. Not all the Jews in Babylon returned to Palestine in the sixth century BCE or thereafter; many of them stayed and became the foundation of a thriving Jewish community there.

2. Many Jews emigrated from Palestine to Egypt and elsewhere in the Mediterranean area, especially after the fourth century BCE. As the array of synagogues mentioned in the book of Acts suggests, by the turn of the era there were Jewish communities across Asia Minor, Greece, and Rome.

3. The Jewish community in Palestine suffered terribly in the second century BCE from the persecutions of the pagan Syrian overlords, the Seleucids. This is the context of the Maccabean uprising, reflected indirectly in the book of Daniel.

4. The Palestinian Jewish community suffered even more from uprisings against Roman occupation in 68–70 CE

and in 132–135 CE, and its population in Palestine thereafter dwindled.

5. In the course of the Middle Ages Jewish communities not only maintained themselves in the ancient world—Babylon and Egypt, Greece and Rome—but spread northward across Europe into Spain and southern France, and later into the Rhine valley and eastward into Poland and beyond. Throughout this progress they suffered intermittent persecutions from Christians.

6. Jewish communities were established in fresh areas of the world, notably in the New World, as part of general European settlements there. One thinks of the large-scale Jewish immigration into the United States in the last few decades of the nineteenth century and the first years of the twentieth century.

7. The movement of Jews back into Palestine gained momentum in the last part of the nineteenth century and especially in the twentieth century under the stimulus of Zionism culminating in the establishment of the state of Israel in 1948.

Now in this chapter I shall treat eight categories of material bearing on Isaiah, several of which developed side by side in the course of the centuries:

- two ancient Jewish translations of the Scriptures, one into Greek (the Septuagint) and one into Aramaic (the Targum)

- literary works that claimed Scriptural status, though finally rejected by the Jewish communities

- the Dead Sea Scrolls

- the Jewish historian Josephus

- the selection of prophetic readings for Sabbaths, feast days and the like (the *haftarot*)

- rabbinic literature, climaxed in the Talmud

- the great medieval commentaries on Jewish Scripture, such as those by Rashi

- Jewish study on Isaiah, alongside parallel Christian study, during the past century

TWO ANCIENT JEWISH TRANSLATIONS OF THE SCRIPTURES

The Jews in Greek-speaking areas had been losing their grip on Hebrew, and a translation into the language they knew became a necessity. Accordingly the Jewish community in Alexandria, Egypt, produced such a translation, which we know as the Septuagint. The work was done little-by-little over many decades so that the book of Isaiah was probably translated by 200 BCE. It was the Septuagint from which the New Testament writers generally drew for their Old Testament quotations, since those writers were writing in Greek.

Every translation is to some extent an interpretation, so in the details of this translation we may discern the earliest Jewish interpretation of Isaiah. Here we see their perception of the meaning of old words in a fresh cultural context.[1]

I shall offer two examples. The first is Isaiah 6:10. We discussed this difficult verse in Chapter 2. God tells Isaiah to "Make the mind of this people dull, and stop their ears, and shut their eyes." In this passage God seems monstrous. The Septuagint has shifted the phrasing; it reads,

"The heart of this people has become dull, and their ears are hard of hearing, and they have shut their eyes"[2] This is the way Matthew cites the verse (see Matthew13:15). In this rendering the impetus does not come from God but rather from the people.

The second example is the Greek translation of the Hebrew verb "created" in four passages of Second Isaiah—40:26, 41:20, 43:15, and 45:18. In these passages the Hebrew was not rendered with a verb like "create" or "make" but rather with one meaning "exhibit, display." For example, 40:26 reads, "Lift up your eyes on high, and see, who has displayed all these things?" Now the Stoic philosophers, such as Epictetus and Plutarch, understood the world to be a spectacle made by the gods for human beings. They depicted the world as something made for human beings to see, interpret, and experience. The Jewish translator of Isaiah, living in the context of Greek philosophical discussion, was aware of this notion but has turned it upside down, depicting the world from God's point of view. If the world is a spectacle, then it is *God* who has displayed the spectacle of the world.[3]

The other Jewish translation of Isaiah from ancient times is even more interpretive than the Septuagint, and this is the Targum.[4] The Targum is the traditional rendering of the Hebrew into Aramaic. Aramaic was a sister language to Hebrew, perhaps as close to Hebrew as Portuguese is to Spanish, or as Dutch is to German. Jews began to shift their speech from Hebrew to Aramaic while they were exiles in Babylon in the time of Second Isaiah, since Aramaic was the *lingua franca* of Babylon. As a result synagogue interpreters began to turn the verses of Hebrew Scripture into Aramaic so that common people could follow the meaning of what they heard. This may be the implication of Nehemiah 8:8, for instance.

Though the practice of Aramaic translation must have begun very early, the text of such a translation that is preserved to our day was evidently stabilized only in the period after Rome destroyed Jerusalem in 70 CE. Nevertheless it is convenient to offer it at this point in our discussion.

In the case of Isaiah and other prophetic books, the Targum was often more of a paraphrase than a word-for-word rendering, so again it allows us a window into early Jewish interpretation.[5] I offer two examples.

In Chapter 2 we discussed the call of Isaiah, which begins, "In the year that King Uzziah died, I saw the Lord sitting on a throne" (6:1), and I noted the difficulty presented by this description in light of God's word to Moses in Exodus 33:20, "No one shall see me and live." The Targum softens Isaiah's description. Here is the way it renders the beginning of the prophet's call: "In the year that King Uzziah was struck with it [that is, leprosy], the prophet said, I saw the glory of the Lord sitting on his throne."[6]

In the fourth Servant Song, 52:13–53:12, the Targum interprets the servant partly as the coming Messiah and partly as Israel. Thus in 53:10, where the Hebrew says, "He shall see his offspring, and shall prolong his days; through him the will of the LORD shall prosper," the Targum offers a long paraphrase: "They shall see the kingdom of their Messiah, they shall increase sons and daughters, they shall prolong days; those who perform the law of the LORD shall prosper in his pleasure."[7]

The Septuagint and the Targum thus offer windows through which we may glimpse the understanding of Isaiah in two contrasting Jewish communities roughly twenty centuries ago.

PSEUDO-SCRIPTURAL WORKS

As I have already indicated, the Palestinian Jewish community underwent terrible persecution at the hands of the Syrian authorities in the early second century BCE, and this persecution stimulated renewed literary activity. The biblical book of Daniel was composed during this period, but there were many other compositions produced at that time that, though claiming Scriptural status, were not in the end accepted as Scripture in the Jewish canon. Among these works are some that have survived to our day, particular through various Christian communities, and in this literature one can often discern the impact of the book of Isaiah. I offer three examples.

The first is the *Martyrdom and Ascension of Isaiah*, preserved particularly within the Ethiopic church.[8] Of eleven chapters, the first five, of Jewish origin, set forth a legend of the martyrdom of Isaiah at the instigation of the wicked King Manasseh (2 Kings 21:1–18). According to this legend, Isaiah met his death by being sawn in two. It is this legend that doubtless lies behind that curious phrase in Hebrews 11:37.

The second is the *Lives of the Prophets*, a Jewish work from the first century CE.[9] Its subtitle summarizes it: "The names of the prophets, and where they are from, and where they died and how, and where they lie." It opens with a section on Isaiah, repeating the legend that he was sawn in two and stating that his tomb is in Jerusalem "near the tomb of the kings."

The third is 4 Maccabees, a Jewish work deeply influenced by Stoic philosophy; this book has twilight status in the Christian canon, being relegated to an appendix in the Septuagint translation.[10] The author, during the last few decades BCE or the first few decades CE, ponders the traditional story (2 Maccabees. 6:12–7:42) of a Jewish mother who, during the Seleucid persecutions, endured the martyrdom of her seven sons. In 4 Maccabees 18:14 the mother describes her husband, who had taught their sons the words of Isaiah, "Even though you go through the fire, the flame shall not consume you" (Isaiah 43:2).

THE DEAD SEA SCROLLS

In Chapter 1, I made brief mention of the Dead Sea Scrolls, in particular the biblical commentaries and references among them. By now almost everyone has heard of these manuscripts and fragments of manuscripts which came to light in the late 1940s and early 1950s from eleven caves south of Jericho. These manuscripts belonged to an apocalyptic Jewish community. They were copied during the period from about 225 BCE to the time of the destruction of the community in 68 CE. The discovery of this material, beginning in 1947–48, and its subsequent publication and study, marks it as the most astonishing and most important biblical archeological find of modern times.[11]

Premier among the scrolls from the first trove, found in Cave 1, is the great Isaiah scroll,[12] the Hebrew text of the whole book of Isaiah on parchment (with a few tiny gaps, mostly from slivers lost on the bottom edge). The scroll is over seven meters (twenty-four feet) long, in fifty-four columns, with letter-forms that date this scroll to about 100 BCE. It is astonishing that a copy of the book of Isaiah has been preserved to our own day from a time only six hundred years after the death of the original Isaiah himself.[13] It should be added that many other fragments of Isaiah have also turned up among the scroll remains.[14]

Beyond text of the biblical book itself, the text of Isaiah had a great influence upon the literature produced by the sect.[15] Thus, as I mentioned in Chapter 1, members of the group prepared commentary material on the text of Isaiah, though unfortunately these texts have survived only in fragments.

More than once in various literary works of the sect Isaiah is cited by name. For example, in one form of the Community Rule, the *Damascus Document*, we read:[16]

> But . . . when God visits the earth in order to empty over them the punishment of the wicked, when there comes the word which is written in the words of Isaiah, son of Amoz, the prophet, which says: "There shall come upon you, upon your people and upon your father's house, days such as have not come since the day Ephraim departed from Judah" [Isaiah 7:17]. When the two houses of Israel separated, Ephraim detached itself from Judah, and all the renegades were delivered up to the sword; but those who remained steadfast escaped to the land of the north.

Beyond specific citations, however, the quantity of reminiscences on passages of Isaiah within the sectarian texts suggests how deeply this prophetic book entered into the thought-world of the community. Here, for example, is a portion of a prayer intended for community use:[17]

> For you have poured your holy spirit upon us [compare Isaiah 44:3] to fill us with your blessings, so that we would look for you in our anguish, and whisper in the grief of your reproach. We are coming into anguish, we were struck and tested by the anger of the oppressor [51:13]; for we too have wearied God by our sins, we have wearied the Rock with our failings [43:24].

But for our profit you did not enslave us away from
our paths [43:23: "burden" in the NRSV is literally
"enslave"], on the.path on which we were obliged to
walk [48:17]. But we did not pay attention to your precepts [48:18].

THE JEWISH HISTORIAN JOSEPHUS

Flavius Josephus, a pro-Roman Jewish historian who
wrote in Greek, was born in 37/38 CE and died sometime
after 100. Of his works, it is the *Jewish Antiquities* that is
relevant to our interest here.[18] In it he paraphrases material from the Old Testament (which he knew in the Septuagint version), supplementing it with other tradition,
both historical and legendary.

He refers to Isaiah, but he curiously downgrades the
importance of that prophet in comparison, for example,
with Jeremiah. One reason for this may have been that
Isaiah had counseled King Hezekiah to resist Assyria
(Isaiah 37), whereas Jeremiah, a hundred years later,
had counseled King Zedekiah to surrender to Babylon
(Jeremiah 37–38). Since Josephus was convinced that
it was hopeless for his fellow-Jews to oppose Rome, he
would naturally have favored the outlook of Jeremiah.[19]
Nevertheless it is thought-provoking to read his statement that Cyrus, king of Persia, was moved to allow the
Jews to return from Babylon to Jerusalem because he
himself had read Isaiah's prophecy, written one hundred
and forty years before the temple was demolished (*Ant.*
11.1.1–2)—Josephus, of course, took it for granted that
the whole book was the work of the original Isaiah, so
the miracle of such prophecy was to him altogether
convincing.

HAFTAROT READINGS

I turn now to the sequence of traditional readings of the prophets in synagogue liturgy. The development of stated readings for each sabbath, as well as those for special holidays, are altogether analogous to the development of Christian lectionaries. The tradition of these readings has come down from ancient times. The entire Pentateuch (Genesis through Deuteronomy) is heard in the course of a year, and various passages of the prophets (the *haftarot*, literally "conclusions," singular *haftarah*) are matched to these Pentateuchal readings. (It is tempting to read the narrative in Luke 4:16–21, in which Jesus reads from the scroll of Isaiah in the synagogue at Nazareth, and understand him on that occasion to be reading a *haftarah*.)

Two matters need to be stressed here. The first is that the prophets, for Jews, comprise the books of Joshua, Judges, Samuel, Kings, Isaiah, Jeremiah, Ezekiel, and the Minor Prophets Hosea through Malachi, so that this list differs at several points from what Christians understand by prophets. The second is that only a selection of texts from the prophets is used.[20]

Matching the weekly readings from the Pentateuch, then, are a selection of readings from the prophets. Of these, fifteen are passages from Isaiah, and five more from Isaiah are used in the services for various holidays. As one surveys the selection two facts strike one immediately. The first is that more *haftarot* readings are taken from Isaiah than from any other prophet.[21] The second is that of these twenty passages, only four are from Isaiah 1–39,[22] the other sixteen being taken from chapters 40–66.[23] That is to say, Jews have manifested the same preference as Christians have for the good news of the last twenty-seven chapters over the mixed message of the first thirty-nine.

A given *haftarah* passage is usually chosen because of
a perceived link to some event described in the Pentateuchal passage just read. For instance, Isaiah 54:1–55:5
is matched with Genesis 6:9–11:32, the narrative of the
flood, because in 54:9 one hears God mention the oath
he swore to Noah. There are other instances in which the
connection is less direct. Thus Isaiah 27:6–28:13 is
matched with Exodus 1:1–6:1 because both Isaiah 27:6
and Exodus 1:5-7 describe the fruitfulness of Jacob.

RABBINIC LITERATURE

We turn back now to ancient Jewish literature that draws
on Isaiah, specifically to the vast ocean of rabbinic literature that evolved over several centuries after the collapse
of Jewish national hopes in 135 CE. Fully as extensive for
Jews as patristic literature (that is, the works of the
Church Fathers) is for Christians, this body of material
is daunting not only in its quantity but also in its con-
ventions of thinking. In our treatment here of the book
of Isaiah there is opportunity only for the merest hint of
its character.[24] I shall deal with midrash, the Mishna, and
the Babylonian Talmud, in that order.

For the sake of clarity, the words of the rabbinic writer
will appear in standard type, quotations from Scripture
will be set in italic, supplemented where necessary with
brief connective phrases, and references set in standard
type within brackets ([]). Similarly, my own explanatory
material will be bracketed

Midrash

Midrash ("expounding") is a general term referring to free
exposition of Scripture, not only legal exposition but sermonic material as well. Beyond the general use of the
term there are specific books of midrash that evolved in

the early centuries of the Common Era. Of these, I shall examine the work called *Pesiqta deRab Kahana*,[25] a work of twenty-eight sections that offer perspectives on synagogue readings.

Section twenty-one of this work explicates Isaiah 60:1–3, the beginning of the *haftarah* that covers all of chapter 60: "Arise, shine; for your light has come, and the glory of the LORD has risen upon you. For darkness shall cover the earth, and thick darkness the peoples, but the LORD will arise upon you, and his glory will appear over you. Nations shall come to your light, and kings to the brightness of your dawn." We shall examine the first two paragraphs of this section.[26]

The first paragraph of the discussion begins with a citation of a second passage understood to have relevance to 60:1–3, namely Isaiah 24:15: "Therefore in the east give glory to the LORD; in the coastlands of the sea glory in the name of the LORD, the God of Israel. The paragraph continues:

> With what do people honor him? With lights. [In the opening clause of 24:15 the translation "in the east" is one interpretation of a strange expression, since the Hebrew text says literally "in the lights" or "with lights." The traditional explanation of this expression is "in the region of light," but present-day scholars wonder whether the text is not actually a copyist's mistake.] Rabbi Abbahu said, "With two lights: *And God made the two great lights* [Genesis 1:16]. How so? When the sun shines, people recite a blessing over it. When the moon comes out, people make a blessing over it." And rabbis say, Said the Holy One, blessed be He, to Israel, 'My children, since my light is your light and your light is my light, let us—both you and I—together go and give light to Zion: *Arise, shine, for your light has come* . . . '" [The discussion underlines the notion that both God and Israel bring light back to Zion.]

The second paragraph proposes Isaiah 42:8 to shed light on 60:1–3:

> Rabbi Aha opened discourse by citing this verse, *I am the* LORD, *that is my name* [Isaiah 42:8]: "[God says,] 'That is the name that the first Man gave to me [a reference to the name "Yahweh," the LORD, Genesis 4:26], that is the name for which I stipulated to myself [Exodus 3:13-15], that is the name for which I stipulated with the ministering angels [compare Isaiah 6:2-3].'" *My glory I give to no other god* [Isaiah42:8]; Rabbi Menahama in the name of Rabbi Abin [said], "This ['god'] refers to the *seirim* [the term occurs in Leviticus 17:7, there translated "goat-demons."]. *Nor my praise to idols* [Isaiah 42:8]: said the Holy One, blessed be He, 'My glory I shall not give to another, but you give my praise to idols. To whom shall I give it? To Zion: *Arise, shine, for your light is come* [Isaiah 60:1].'"

This paragraph offers the notion that God gives glory to Zion even while the Israelites assign it to things of this world.

MISHNA

I turn now to the Mishna ("repetition"). This work is a compilation of oral tradition on all aspects of Jewish law that had been collected by about 200 CE. The designation of "repetition" refers to the *oral* opinions on the law alongside the law in *written* Scripture.[27] The standard translation of the Mishna into English covers eight hundred pages.[28] The greatest number of citations in this work are naturally to passages of law in the Pentateuch. Even so, in the course of its discussions there are citations to other parts of the Bible, including Isaiah, and it is instructive to see how the rabbis of this epoch used Isaiah in their exposition of the law. I shall offer two examples.

In regard to the goat sent into the wilderness on the Day of Atonement (Leviticus 16:8, 10, 26), the question arises:

> Whence do we learn that they tie a strip of crimson on the head of the scapegoat? Because it is written, *Though your sins be as scarlet they shall be as white as snow* [Isaiah 1:18].[29]

Again, in a discussion of what crafts a father should teach his son, Rabbi Nehorai (who flourished around 150 CE) says:

> I would set aside all the crafts in the world and teach my son naught save the Law. But with all other crafts it is not so; for when a man falls into sickness or old age or troubles and cannot engage in his work, lo, he dies of hunger. But with the Law it is not so; for it guards him from all evil while he is young, and in old age it grants him a future and a hope. Of his youth, what does it say? *They that wait upon the LORD shall renew their strength* [Isaiah 40:31]. Of his old age what does it say? *They shall still bring forth fruit in old age* [Ps. 92:14].[30]

THE BABYLONIAN TALMUD

In the centuries after the compilation of the Mishna, the rabbis made two compilations of commentary on the Mishna, both called Talmud (literally "learning, study"), the Talmud of the Land of Israel and the Talmud of Babylonia. Of these the latter is the more extensive.[31] The Babylonian Talmud, completed by the middle of the sixth century CE, covers many volumes and consists of legal and sermonic material. It is difficult to cite an example dealing with Isaiah that both gives a sense of the rabbinic discourse of those centuries and at the same time can

be made explicable to readers outside that tradition, but
let us try with the following.

> *Therefore shall the Lord, the Lord of hosts, send among
> his fat ones leanness* [Isaiah 10:16]. [*The NRSV trans-
> lates "wasting sickness among his stout warriors."*] What
> is *among his fat ones* [Hebrew: *bemishmanaw*] *leanness?*
> Said the Holy One, blessed be He, Let Hezekiah
> come, who has eight [Hebrew: *shemoneh*] names, and
> exact punishment from Sennacherib, who has eight
> names [likewise]. [That is, the Hebrew for "fat ones"
> is associated with "eight" by the same consonant
> sequence sh-m-n.]
>   As to Hezekiah, it is written, *For unto us a child
> is born, unto us a son is given; and the government shall
> be upon his shoulder: and his name shall be called* [1]
> *Wonderful,* [2] *Counselor,* [3] *Mighty,* [4] *Judge* [this
> translation of the Hebrew word for "God" as "Judge"
> is derived from passages like Exodus 21:6], [5] *Ever-
> lasting,* [6] *Father,* [7] *Prince,* and [8] *Peace* [the
> Hebrew phrase can allow the omission of "of."]. And
> there is yet the name 'Hezekiah' too [That is, there is
> a ninth name.]. [Hezekiah] means, "Whom God has
> strengthened." Another matter [that is, alternatively]:
> it is 'Hezekiah,' for he strengthened Israel [in their
> devotion] for their Father in Heaven. [That is to say,
> two explanations are offered for the meaning of the
> name "Hezekiah," taken here not as a proper name but
> as an epithet with two parts: Hebrew hazak "be strong"
> and *Yah* (the name of God).]
>   As to Sennacherib, it is written, [1] *Tiglath-pileser*
> [2 Kings 15:29], [2] [*Tiglath-*]*Pilneser* [1 Chron. 5:26],
> [3] *Shalmaneser* [2 Kings 17:3], [4] *Pul* [1 Chron.
> 5:26], [5] *Sargon* [Isaiah 20:1], [6] *Asnapper* [NSRV
> Osnappar] [Ezra 4:10], [7] *Rabba* [Aramaic for "great"]
> [Ezra 4:10], [8] *Yaqqira* [Aramaic for "noble"] [Ezra
> 4:10] [The phrase is taken here to be three proper
> names.]. And there is yet the name 'Sennacherib' too
> [that is, there is a ninth name.]. It bears the sense that
> his conversation was contentious. Another matter [that

is, alternatively]: he talked and babbled against the Most High. [That is, two explanations are offered for Sennacherib's name, again taken not as a proper name but as an epithet with three parts: Hebrew *syh* "*converse*," *nahar* "stab," and *rib* "strife."]

The author of this comment has taken as a single identification five different Assyrian kings— Tiglath-pileser III (745–727), Shalmaneser V (726–722), Sargon II (721–705), Sennacherib (704–681), and Asshurbanipal (668–627)—evidently because the first four made war on Israel or Judah, and the fifth settled deported populations in Samaria. "Tiglath-pilneser" and "Pul" are both alternatives for Tiglath-pileser. "Osnappar," Ezra 4:10, evidently refers to Assurbanipal, but it is striking that some manuscripts of the Septuagint of Ezra 4:10 read "Shalmaneser," and that in this context Josephus (*Ant.* 11.2.1) likewise refers to Shalmaneser. Clearly then, in later centuries confusion was possible over the various Assyrian kings.

The author has also offered real or presumed derivations for the names "Hezekiah" and "Sennacherib." The first derivation of Hezekiah is sound ("the LORD strengthens"), since it is a Hebrew name, but the derivations of Sennacherib are folk etymologies in Hebrew, since, of course, the name is Assyrian.

To summarize: the rabbis have associated "fat ones" with "eight. " Understanding the royal designations in Isaiah 9:6 to refer to Hezekiah, they have taken those designations as eight names and have matched them with eight names presumed to refer to Sennacherib. This passage, a complex and imaginative association of texts and words, affords a modest insight into modes of rabbinic thinking during the early centuries of the common era, modes of thinking saturated with biblical material.

MEDIEVAL BIBLICAL COMMENTARIES

In the centuries that followed, various cultural factors shifted the attention of Jewish scholars away from imaginative association toward careful etymological and grammatical rigor in explaining texts. These scholars produced noteworthy commentaries on Scripture.[32] Of the commentaries on Isaiah, three loom large for us, that of Solomon ben Isaac, usually known by his Hebrew acronym Rashi; that of Abraham ibn Ezra; and that of David Kimhi (often spelled Kimchi or Qimhi).[33]

Rashi (1040–1105 CE) lived his whole life in Troyes, in the southern part of the province of Champagne, southeast of Paris. For Jews his commentaries, direct, simple, and often homely, have been the most popular. One curiosity of Rashi's commentaries is that he often defines rare Hebrew words by the equivalents in the French current in his day. These "glosses," recorded in the Hebrew alphabet, are among the oldest relics of Old French to come down to us. Thus when dealing with Isaiah 2:20 he defines the Hebrew word for "bats" with the note, "in the vernacular, *qylb' swryz*." This is his transcription of the Old French *chalve soriz*, the modern French *chauve-souris*.[34]

In his comment on Isaiah 53:3 he understands the suffering servant to be not one individual, but the entire people of Israel. "It is the way of this prophet to address all of Israel as if it were one man [as in, for example], *Do not fear, O Jacob my servant* [44:2]." And the remarks in his commentary on 53:9 could well reflect the agony the Jews experienced in his own day—the Crusades to Palestine were just getting underway, and many Jews were tortured and killed by hysterical Christian mobs:

> *They made his grave with the wicked and his tomb with the rich, although he has done no violence, and there*

was no deceit in his mouth [53:9]. He delivered himself to be buried in whatever manner the evil idol worshipers decreed, who inflicted upon them killing, and a donkey's burial [compare Jeremiah 22:19] in a dog's grave [that is, in utter humiliation]. In keeping with the decision of the evil ones he was willing to be buried [in this manner] and did not deny the living God. In keeping with the decision of the ruling authority he had delivered himself up to every kind of death which he [the former] decreed [for him] because he did not want to take it upon himself to do evil and to commit violence, as was done by the idol worshipers in whose midst he had lived.[35]

Ibn Ezra (1092–1167 CE) was born in Toledo, Spain. He had a wide-ranging intellect and traveled widely as well. He is remembered as a poet, scientist, and philosopher, as well as a grammarian and biblical commentator. If Rashi offered definitions in Old French, ibn Ezra often cited Arabic cognates. Arabic and Hebrew are related Semitic languages, and Toledo, part of a Moorish (Muslim) kingdom in his day, was a center of Arabic and Hebrew learning.[36] Here are a few samples of his comments.

In the year that King Uzziah died [Isaiah 6:1]. Our sages said that "died" here is used for "became a leper" [compare the rendering, cited above, of the Targum on this verse]; for when Uzziah entered the temple to offer the incense [2 Chronicles 26:20–21], the earthquake took place. [There is an earthquake mentioned in Amos 1:1, and some Jewish traditions associate "the pivots on the thresholds shook," v. 4, with this earthquake.] This may be true, but "died" can also be taken literally; in that case the death of Uzziah must be placed in the same year in which Isaiah became prophet; no objection can beraised from [the phrasing of] *in the days of Uzziah* [1:1], since even months might have passed between Isaiah's initiation as prophet and the death of Uzziah.

In his discussion of 6:8 Abraham ibn Ezra deals wth two issues.

> *For us.* He speaks now to the seraphim; therefore he says, "for us" [plural; compare my remarks on the passage in Chapter 2]. *Here am I, send me.* [The prophet implies,] Since my lips are pure, I am fit to be the messenger, but I was not before. From these words I infer that this chapter contains Isaiah's first prophecy [in spite of the fact that five chapters precede the passage].

Though he used guarded language, Abraham ibn Ezra evidently doubted that chapters 40–66 were the work of the original Isaiah in the eighth century, and in this doubt he was a precursor of modern scholarly opinion. He begins his comment on chapter 40 this way:

> This chapter has been placed here for the following reason: in the preceding chapter it is predicted that all the treasures of the King, and even his sons, will be carried away to Babylon [39:6–7: modern scholars conclude that these verses are the work of redactors in the early sixth century]; this sad prediction is properly followed by the words of comfort. These first comforting promises, with which the second part of the book of Isaiah begins, refer, as Rabbi Moses Hakkohen believes, to the restoration of the temple by Zerubbabel [in 520–515 BCE]; according to my opinion to the coming redemption from our present exile. Prophecies concerning the Babylonian exile are introduced only as an illustration.

This remark is based on the assumption that the prophecies in chapters 40–66 were announced either after the end of the Babylonian exile, or at least immediately before the fall of Babylon, when the coming events could already be seen by everyone. These words would then be a cogent argument for Jews in his own day to be strengthened in their faith in the fulfillment of prophecies of the coming Messiah.

David Kimhi (1160–1235 CE) lived in Narbonne, a city in Provence (southwestern France) near the Mediterranean Sea.[37] Like Abraham ibn Ezra, his method was heavily biased toward the basic work of grammar and dictionary meanings. With regard to the problematic clause in 6:1, "I saw the Lord," first he cites the renderings of two passages in the Aramaic Targum. The first is the one under discussion, where, as we have seen, the Targum renders, "The glory of the LORD." The second is Exodus 19:20, where the Hebrew text says, baldly, "When the LORD descended upon Mount Sinai." There the Targum softens the text to "And the LORD was revealed on Mount Sinai," which he cites as "And the glory of the LORD was revealed."[38] Then goes on to cite the Hebrew text of Ezek. 1:26, part of Ezekiel's vision of God, which reads, "And seated above the likeness of a throne was something that seemed like a human form." On all this he comments:

> Our rabbis, of blessed memory, found the [two] verses difficult: they said, it is written, for *no one can see me and live* [Exodus 33:20],and [at the same time] it is written [in the passage under discussion], *I saw the Lord*—in one place, in an evil image, and another place in a non-evil image. [That is to say, the rabbis maintained that these expressions cannot both be benign.] But our rabbis, of blessed memory, [also] said, "Everything that Ezekiel saw, Isaiah saw." [Are we to say that] Ezekiel is to be compared to a boy denying that he saw the king, [while] Isaiah is to be compared to a boy insisting that he saw the king? [No.] More specifically, Ezekiel told verbally explicit statements, because it was a great novelty [either] for him or for

the children of his generation, but Isaiah did not tell
[his vision] except by means of a generality.

Kimhi is denying two contentions at the same time.
On the one hand he denies that there is a crucial con-
tradiction between Isaiah's "I saw the Lord" and the
statement in Exodus that "no one can see me and live."
It is not simply true that one description is evil while the
other is benign. On the other hand he denies that Ezekiel's
description, the traditional answer to the Isaiah dilemma,
is in absolute contrast to Isaiah's description.

With regard to the command to Isaiah in 6:9, "Go and
say to this people: 'Keep listening, but do not comprehend;
keep looking, but do not understand,'" a command which
appears to make God monstrous, Kimhi remarks,

> It is a judgment and a sentence from God (may he be
> blessed), as though he should desire anyone to sin
> against the Holy One (blessed be he)! He has with-
> held from him [the sinner] the ways of repentance
> until he accepts his penalty." He then cites parallels—
> the repeated statement in Exodus 7–9 that God would
> harden Pharaoh's heart; Deuteronomy 2:30, "For the
> LORD your God has hardened his [Sihon's] spirit," and
> 1 Samuel 2:25, "But they [the sons of Eli] would not
> listen to the voice of their father; for it was the will of
> the LORD to kill them.

THE CURRENT CONVERGENCE OF JEWISH
AND CHRISTIAN WORK ON ISAIAH

In our own century we see a strikingly fresh development
as Jewish and Christian scholars mutually enrich each
other in matters bearing on the Old Testament. From a
large host of Jewish scholars I must offer only a single, towering example, Harry M. Orlinsky (1908-92). Orlinsky was

born in Toronto. He was a professor for many years at the Hebrew Union College–Jewish Institute of Religion in New York. In 1945 he joined the translation committee sponsored by the National Council of Churches that produced the Revised Standard Version (1952), and he continued on that committee during the whole preparation of the New Revised Standard Version (1989). At the same time he was editor-in-chief of the new translation of the Hebrew Scriptures for the Jewish Publication Society (1962–82).[39] His publications were voluminous. Those bearing on Isaiah include an article in 1950 on the great scroll of Isaiah among the Dead Sea Scrolls,[40] the article on "Virgin" in the *Interpreter's Dictionary of the Bible, Supplementary Volume*,[41] and a long monograph, "The So-Called 'Servant of the Lord' and 'Suffering Servant' in Second Isaiah" (1977).[42] Orlinsky's work continues to serve both Jewish and Christian communities.

The material surveyed in this chapter gives only the *barest* hint of the richness of Jewish work on the text of Isaiah through the centuries, work both on the meaning and on the implications of the text. We can rejoice at the happy development of the convergence in our day of Jewish and Christian work on our common Scriptures, especially given the long and horrid history of Christian persecution of Jews and of mutual misunderstanding and mistrust.

NOTES

1. For a convenient though uncritical translation of the Septuagint into English see *The Septuagint Version of the Old Testament: With an English Translation* (London: Samuel Bagster). Various editions of this work were published from 1844 to the end of the nineteenth century.

2. The example is that of Johan Lust, "The Demonic Character of Jahweh and the Septuagint of Isaiah," *Bijdragen* 40 (1979), 13, cited in Stanley E. Porter and Brook W. R. Pearson, "Isaiah Through Greek

Eyes: The Septuagint of Isaiah," in Craig C. Broyles and Craig A. Evans (eds.), *Writing and Reading the Scroll of Isaiah, Studies of an Interpretive Tradition* (Supplements to Vetus Testamentum 70; Leiden: Brill, 1997), 538.

3. Porter and Pearson, 537.

4. There were actually several Targums; the official Targum on the Prophets is the Targum Jonathan (bar-Uzziel).

5. For a translation into English of the Targum on Isaiah see *The Aramaic Bible: The Targums*, Vol. 11, *The Isaiah Targum*, ed. Bruce D. Chilton (Wilmington, DE: Michael Glazier, 1987).

6. Bruce D. Chilton, "Two in One: Renderings of the Book of Isaiah in Targum Jonathan," in *Writing and Reading the Scroll of Isaiah, Studies of an Interpretive Tradition*, (ed. Craig C. Boyles and Craig A. Evans; Supplements to Vetus Testamentum 70; Leiden, 1997), 559.

7. Ibid., 555–56.

8. Michael A. Knibb, "Martyrdom and Ascension of Isaiah," in Vol. 2 of *The Old Testament Pseudepigrapha*, (James Charlesworth, Garden City, NY: Doubleday, 1985), 143–64.

9. D. R. A. Hare, "The Lives of the Prophets," in Vol. 2 of *The Old Testament Pseudepigrapha*, (James Charlesworth, Garden City, NY: Doubleday, 1985), 379–86.

10. The book of 4 Maccabees may be found in editions of the New Revised Standard Version with the Apocryphal/Deuterocanonical Books; see further H. Anderson, "4 Maccabees," in *The Old Testament Pseudepigrapha*, (James Charlesworth, Garden City, NY: Doubleday, 1985), 531–64.

11. The literature on the scrolls is huge. The fullest and most authoritative edition of the sectarian texts (that is, texts other than copies of biblical books) is now Florentino García Martínez, *The Dead Sea Scrolls Translated* (Leiden: Brill, 1994).

12. Its designation is 1QIs^a.

13. There is a handsome edition of a complete set of photographs of this scroll: *Scrolls from Qumrân Cave I* (Jerusalem: The Albright Institute of Archaeological Research and The Shrine of the Book, 1972).

14. Eugene Ulrich, "An Index to the Contents of the Isaiah Manuscripts from the Judean Desert,"in *Writing and Reading the Scroll of Isaiah Studies of an Interpretive Tradition* (ed. Craig C. Broyles and Craig A. Evans; Supplements to the Vetus Testamentum 70; Leiden:

Brill, 1997), 477–80.

15. On the whole topic see George J. Brooks, "Isaiah in the Pesharim and Other Qumran Texts," in Broyles and Evans, op. cit., 609-32.

16. The passage is CD-A VII.9-14, cited from García Martínez, op. cit., 37. The references to chapter and verse within brackets in this citation and subsequent citations are of course modern. This particular text, interestingly, was preserved in a storeroom of a Cairo synagogue and discovered in 1896; only after the discovery of the Scrolls from the Dead Sea did it become clear to scholars that it is actually a text from the same community.

17. The passage is 4Q504 (4QDibHam^a=4QWords of the Luminaries^a) V.15-21; see García Martínez, op. cit., 415. There are a few gaps in the text, filled in by the editors, that I have not indicated. For the reminiscences of Isaiah compare J. Carmignac, É. Cothenet and H. Lignée, Les Textes de Qumran, 2 (Paris: Letouzey et Ané, 1963) 306-307.

18. This work has often been translated and published. The best recent edition is Flavius Josephus, Jewish Antiquities, with an English Translation by H. St. J. Thackeray and Ralph Marcus (Loeb Classical Library; New York: Putnam, 1926-; repr. Cambridge, MA: Harvard University Press).

19. Louis H. Feldman, "Josephus' Portrait of Isaiah," in Writing and Reading the Scroll of Isaiah Studies of an Interpretive Tradition (ed. Craig C. Broyles and Craig A. Evans; Supplements to the Vetus Testamentum 70; Leiden: Brill, 1997), 583–608, esp. 592–96.

20. I. George Dobsevage, "Haftarah," The Jewish Encyclopedia 6:135–37.

21. Feldman, "Josephus' Portrait of Isaiah," 588.

22. Isaiah 1:1–27; 6:1–7:6; 10:32–12:6; 27:6–28:13.

23. Isaiah 40:1–26; 40:27–41:16; 42:5–43:10; 43:21–44:23; 49:14–51:4; 51:12–52:13; 54:1–55:5; 54:1–10; 54:11–55:6; 55:6–8; 55:6–56:8; 57:14–58:14; 60:1–22; 61:10–63:9; 66:1–24.

24. A useful recent treatment of this literature is Jacob Neusner, Introduction to Rabbinic Literature (The Anchor Bible Reference Library; New York: Doubleday, 1994). For Isaiah a useful survey is Gary A. Porton, "Isaiah and the Kings: The Rabbis on the Prophet Isaiah," in Writing and Reading the Scroll of Isaiah Studies of an Interpretive Tradition (ed. Craig C. Broyles and Craig A. Evans; Supplements to the Vetus Testamentum 70; Leiden: Brill, 1997), 693-716.

25. Neusner, 411–33.

26. For the passage see Jacob Neusner (translator), *Pesiqta deRab Kahana, An Analytical Translation* 2 (Brown Judaic Studies 123; Atlanta: Scholars Press, 1987) 71-72.

27. Neusner, *Rabbinic Literature*, 97–128.

28. Herbert Danby, *The Mishnah* (Oxford: Oxford University Press, 1993).

29. *m. Šabbat* 9.3; see Danby, 108; compare *m. Yoma* 6;8, see Danby, 170.

30. *m. Qiddušin* 4.14; see Danby, 329.

31. Neusner, *Rabbinic Literature*, 153–220.

32. See in general Erwin I. J. Rosenthal, "The Study of the Bible in Medieval Judaism," in *The Cambridge History of the Bible*, 2 (ed. G. W. H. Lampe, Cambridge: Cambridge University Press, 1969), 252–79.

33. Unfortunately the commentaries on Isaiah written by these scholars are relatively inaccessible. The book of Isaiah in the traditional Jewish *Mikra'ot Gedolot* (Scriptures with commentaries) includes the Hebrew text of Rashi and Kimhi but not of Ibn Ezra, and (if I may make a personal observation) the display of the Hebrew text of the commentaries in minuscule "Rashi script" does not make easy reading. See *Mikra'ot Gedolot* (Warsaw, 1874–77; repr. New York: Pardes, 1951), Vol. 8. Translations of the commentaries are spotty: see the notes below.

34. The *y* in *qylb'* apears to be a copyist's error. For this gloss see David S. Blondheim, *Les Gloses Françaises dans les Commentaires Talmudiques de Raschi*, 2 (The Johns Hopkins Studies in Romance Literatures and Languages, Extra Volume 11; Baltimore: Johns Hopkins; London: Oxford University Press, 1937), 142. There is an earlier (Vulgar Latin) gloss of this word in the plural from the Reichenau glosses (eighth century), *calves sorices*; see Henri F. Muller and Pauline Taylor, *Chrestomathy of Vulgar Latin* (Boston, etc.: D. C. Heath, 1932), 253, #123. The French expression *chauve souris* means 'bald mouse,' but classical Latin *sorex* meant "shrew" rather than "mouse;" and of course the (masculine) plural of *calvus* should be *calvi* rather than *calves*.

35. For Rashi's remarks on 53:3 and 9 see Esra Shereshevsky, *Rashi, The Man and His World* (New York: Sepher-Hermon, 1982), 120, 242–43.

36. There is an English translation of ibn Ezra on Isaiah: Michael

Friedländer, *The Commentary of Ibn Ezra on Isaiah* (London: Trüb-
ner, 1873; repr. New York: Philipp Feldheim, 196).

37. A critical edition of the first part of Kimhi's commentary is: Louis
Finkelstein, *The Commentary of David Kimhi on Isaiah* (Columbia
University Oriental Studies 19; New York: Columbia University Press,
1926; repr. New York: AMS Press, 1966).

38. Interestingly Kimhi misstates himself here. The best texts of the
Targum simply read, "And the LORD was revealed on Mount Sinai;"
see the passage in Alexander Sperber, *The Bible in Aramaic*. (Vol. 1
of *The Tentateuch According to Targum Onkelos*; Leiden: Brill, 1959).

39. *Tanakh: A New Translation of the Holy Scriptures According to the
Traditional Hebrew Text* (Philadelphia: Jewish Publication Society,
1985); repr. of *The Torah*; *The Prophets*; *The Writings* (Philadelphia:
Jewish Publication Society, 1962, 1978, 1982).

40. Harry M. Orlinsky, "Studies in the St. Mark's Isaiah Scroll," *Journal of Biblical Literature* 69 (1950): 149–66.

41. Harry M. Orlinsky, "Virgin," *Interpreter's Dictionary of the Bible,
Supplementary Volume* (Nashville: Abingdon, 1977), 939–40.

42. Harry M. Orlinsky, "The So-Called 'Servant of the Lord' and
'Suffering Servant' in Second Isaiah," in *Studies on the Second Part of
the Book of Isaiah* (Supplements to Vetus Testamentum 14; Leiden:
Brill, 1977), 1–133.

Chapter 8 ——————

The Spirit of the Lord is upon Me: Jesus, the New Testament, and Christian Tradition
(with an afterword on Islam)

WE TURN NOW TO THE Christian tradition in which the New Testament stands as source and center. The New Testament is rich with quotations of and allusions to the book of Isaiah, but a discussion of Isaiah in the New Testament is immensely complicated by four interrelated circumstances, each of them offering its own complications:

1. the New Testament's preoccupation with Jesus of Nazareth;

2. the probability that Jesus himself was particularly drawn to texts from Isaiah 40–66 as he shaped his ministry;

3. the probability that a good portion of the tradition about him, preserved by Jesus' followers was shaped

by their knowledge of Old Testament texts, especially those in Isaiah;

4. the New Testament community's conviction that God's purpose in texts of the Old Testament, notably those in Isaiah, was to point to Jesus Christ.

So stated, none of these circumstances is difficult to understand, but it is important to be clear about the consequences. Let me discuss each of them briefly.

PREOCCUPIED WITH JESUS

The New Testament is utterly preoccupied with one person, Jesus of Nazareth. By contrast, no section of Isaiah is so preoccupied with a given historical person. As we can see, neither the original Isaiah, nor King Ahaz, nor King Hezekiah, nor any specific king of Assyria, is a central preoccupation of chapters 1–35: most of the texts in those chapters are altogether open-ended and thus available for a variety of applications. By the same token, in chapters 40–66 the person of the prophet himself is hidden, and King Cyrus of Persia is mentioned by name only twice (44:28 and 45:1).

To this the New Testament stands in contrast. The historical specificity of Jesus of Nazareth, and the claim of the Christian community that God has acted definitively in this person, take center stage. This contrast is nicely set forth in the first two verses of the Letter to the Hebrews: "Long ago God spoke to our ancestors in many and various ways by the prophets, but in these last days he has spoken to us by a Son, whom he appointed heir of all things, through whom he also created the worlds." For our purposes one would have only to add, after "the prophets," the words "especially Isaiah." Jesus stands like the narrow neck of an hourglass. Through him all the grains of sand pass between past and future. This means that, according to the writers of the New Testament, the texts of Isaiah that are relevant to Christian proclamation point specifically to Jesus Christ and to the experience of the first-century Christian community. The texts of Isaiah are selected, read, and understood in the light of this central conviction.

FORMED BY THE PROPHET'S TEACHING

The second circumstance is that it is altogether probable that Jesus himself was particularly drawn to texts in Isaiah 40–66 in his own formation and then as he shaped his own ministry. I say "probable" because reconstructing the life and teachings of the historical Jesus, an endeavor pursued by many of the most acute biblical scholars of the last century and a half, is a task of daunting complexity. It is common knowledge that the earliest letters of Paul date from the 50s of the first century, and the earliest gospel (Mark) from about 70. Thus it was in oral form that narratives about Jesus circulated for several decades before being fixed in writing. But (to take a signal example), there is nothing intrinsically improbable about the narrative of Jesus' applying the words of Isaiah 61:1–2 to himself during his appearance in the synagogue at Nazareth (Luke 4:16–21). If this is the case, then we must envisage Jesus meditating on many of these texts as he shaped his priorities.

SHAPED BY TRADITION

The third circumstance, one that I suspect is harder for many Christians to accept, is the contrary of the second. Jesus' followers probably shaped a good portion of the shared tradition about him on the basis of prior Old Testament texts, especially those in Isaiah. This is not to accuse the earliest Christians of pious fraud, or of a scheme to "make everything come out right." Rather it is a natural result of the development of oral tradition in a community whose minds were saturated by Old Testament texts.

The Gospel of Matthew is particularly heavy with Old Testament reminiscences. In Matthew 4:12–16 the evangelist explains Jesus' ministry in Capernaum with a reference to "land of Zebulun, land of Naphtali" and to the proclamation that "the people who sat in darkness have seen a great light" (Isaiah 9:1–2). Of course there is no way to know whether Jesus himself thought of this passage during the time when he ministered in Capernaum. Certainly there could be any of a number of factors beyond the words of Isaiah that might lead him to that city. Again there is the well-known reference in Matthew to the virgin birth (Matthew 1:22, citing Isaiah 7:14 in the Septuagint phrasing; compare Luke 1:34). Along with this affirmation one must ponder the fact that there is no record that Jesus himself ever mentioned this circumstance of his birth. There are certainly startling passages that suggest both that the historical Mary did not understand Jesus' mission (Mark 3:31–35) and that Jesus rejected any attempt to exalt her (Luke 11:27–28). What I am proposing is simply that many of the details in the story of Jesus, which was preserved by the New Testament writers, were suggested by the Old Testament texts they had already learned so well.

FORETELLING THE FUTURE

The fourth circumstance is closely related to the first. It is the conviction held by the New Testament writers that the Old Testament texts, preeminently those of Isaiah, were shaped by God specifically to announce the good news of Jesus Christ. For these writers, questions regarding the original historical contexts of the passages, or of any alternative interpretations of the passages, are never at issue. In the context of the gospel, Paul speaks of "the depth of the riches and wisdom and knowledge of God" (Romans 11:33), and after that wonderful phrase he cites Isaiah 40:13, "For who has known the mind of the Lord? Or who has been his counselor?" The New Testament proclaims that the gospel is the very center of the mind of God.

With these interrelated circumstances in mind, let us examine some of the ways the texts of Isaiah appear in the New Testament. First of all there is the sheer number of quotations of and allusions to Isaiah. They are found in almost every book of the New Testament. Only the Pastoral Epistles (1 and 2 Timothy and Titus) and 2 and 3 John lack them. And page for page, no book of the Old Testament is cited in the New Testament more often than Isaiah.[1]

Some of these quotations specifically mention Isaiah. Among these are the citation of Isaiah 61:1–2 in Luke 4:16–21 already mentioned, or the citation of Isaiah 9:1–2 in Matthew 4:15–16. Other quotations, however, are marked only by the vague "as it is written." For example, Isaiah 59:7–9 in Romans 3:15–17 (see v. 10 there). Still others are simply allusions, reminiscences, or echoes, conscious or unconscious, of phrases in Isaiah, such as the words of Isaiah 14:13, 15 that shape Jesus' words about Capernaum in Matthew 11:23 and Luke 10:15. And we must remind ourselves that the wording of material from Isaiah preserved in the New Testament is not always close to the wording familiar to us from the Old Testament. Old Testament citations in the New Testament were normally from the Septuagint translation rather than directly from the original Hebrew, and in any event the words of the citations are often only loosely quoted, as in the citation of Isaiah 59:7–8 in Romans 3:15–17. Most of the citations are used to refer to or describe Jesus Christ, but others are understood to refer more generally to the mighty acts of God, or to Christian experience, as when Paul cites Isaiah 59:20–21 and 27:9 in Romans 11:26–27.

JESUS IN THE SYNOPTIC GOSPELS

Sayings of Jesus which are based on Isaiah are drawn from the whole book. Thus, to give only two examples from Isaiah 1–35, the parable of the vineyard (Mark 12:1–9; Matthew 21:33–40; Luke 20:9–16) is a recasting of the song of the vineyard in Isaiah 5:1–7. And in Mark 7:6–7 and Matthew 15:8–9 we hear, "Well did Isaiah prophesy of you hypocrites, as it is written: 'This people honors me with its lips, but their ear is far from me; in vain do they worship me, teaching as doctrines the precepts of men,'" a citation of Isaiah 29:13.

It is Isaiah 40–66 that is most basic for Jesus' teaching and ministry. Indeed the very notion of gospel, (good news) is clearly derived from the Hebrew term (NRSV "good tidings") that occurs five times in Isaiah 40–66 (40:9; 41:27; 52:7; 60:6; and 61:1). The word gospel itself occurs in the very first verse of the Gospel of Mark. It is of course a universal theme of the New Testament. One of the tasks of the prophet in Isaiah 61:1–2, which Jesus read in the synagogue at Nazareth, was, "He has anointed me to bring good news to the poor."[2]

I shall offer two examples of sayings of Jesus based on antecedents in Isaiah 40–66. Mark 11:17 (also

Matthew 21:13 and Luke 19:46), "Is it not written, 'My house shall be called a house of prayer for all the nations?'" is a citation of Isaiah 56:7, ". . . for my house will be called a house of prayer for all peoples." The beatitude, "Blessed are those who mourn, for they shall be comforted" (Matthew 5:4), is clearly a reflection of a clause of Isaiah 61:2 not cited in the narrative in Luke 4:19 of Jesus' reading from Isaiah, namely, "to comfort all who mourn." A recent authority has stated, "The evidence leads to the conclusion that Jesus' understanding and proclamation of the kingdom of God were grounded in the prophecy of Second Isaiah."[3]

Now we face a central question: Did Jesus of Nazareth consciously understand his own role to be that of the suffering servant? Clearly the New Testament community embraced the identification—we recall Philip's explication of Isaiah 53:7–8 to the Ethiopian eunuch in Acts 8:32–33. Matthew sprinkles his narrative with citations of the Servant passages (Matthew 8:17, citing Isaiah 53:4; Matthew 12:18–21, citing Isaiah 42:1–4). But did the historical Jesus understand himself to undertake that role? Again we can deal only with probabilities. Mark, the earliest gospel, portrays Jesus as altogether conscious of the role. Mark 9:12 suggests Isaiah 53:3 ("despised"), and 10:45 suggests Isaiah 53:11–12. And Mark 14:24, the words over the wine at the Last Supper, are particularly persuasive, recalling Isaiah 53:12 ("poured out," "many"). As we assess the evidence from Mark we must be aware that that evangelist does not have the interest in Jesus' fulfilling Scripture in the way Matthew does. Clearly Jesus saw himself as a prophet of the end-time, offering his people a last chance to repent (Mark 1:15). There is evidence that among Jews in his day there was a growing doctrine of rejected and martyred prophets (compare the phrasing in 4 Maccabees 6:28–29 and 17:22), and Jesus would have had to be aware of the possibility of his own martyrdom.[4] Given these circumstances, and given the centrality of Isaiah 40–66 in his understanding of mission and the prominence of the Servant passages in those chapters, it would be surprising indeed if the reminiscences of Isaiah 53 in Mark's narrative did not go back to Jesus himself.

On the other hand, Mark's narrative of Jesus' citation of Isaiah 6:9–10, that dismaying portion of the call of Isaiah, to explain the opacity of his parables for the crowds at large (Mark 4:12; Matthew 13:13; and Luke 8:10; compare also John 12:40) is probably not authentic to Jesus. A current New Testament scholar has written, "It was the church, not Jesus that used the vocabulary of 'mystery,' saw itself on the 'inside' and everyone else 'outside,' and developed a theory of God's 'hardening' of Israel to explain the relative failure of its mission to the Jews."[5]

REFERENCES IN THE GOSPEL OF JOHN AND IN PAUL'S LETTERS

The Gospel of John offers citations to Isaiah just as the Synoptics do. Thus one may note that in John 1:23, John the Baptist cites Isaiah 40:3 as a reference to himself, while in Mark 1:3 and Matthew 3:3 the evangelists cite the reference themselves. In John 12:38–41 Jesus is portrayed as citing Isaiah 53:1 and 6:9–10 in the context of his rejection by the religious authorities; the first citation is not found in the Synoptics, while the citation of 6:9–10 has a different reference in the Synoptics, as we have seen.

The letters of Paul are rich in citations to Isaiah. Let us explore the matter simply within the Letter to the Romans. Romans 9:20–33 offers a chain of allusions and citations. Thus in Isaiah 45:9 Second Isaiah alludes to

29:16, and the phrasing of both these verses stands behind Romans 9:20, in which Paul raises the rhetorical question whether anyone should argue with the logic of God. In Romans 9:27–28 Paul directly cites most of Isaiah 10:22–23, and in Romans 9:29 he cites Isaiah 1:9, in all of which he is arguing that God never intended to save all the Israelites. Then in Romans 9:32–33 he alludes to Isaiah 8:14 and cites more directly 28:16. For him the "stone of stumbling" is Jesus Christ.

There are in Romans several references to the Servant passages as descriptions of Jesus and the gospel, a light allusion to Isaiah 50:8 in Romans 8:33, and more substantial allusions to 53:12 in Romans 4:25 and to 52:15 in Romans 15:21. Paul also alludes to Christ's ministry of salvation to Israel in Romans 11:26–27, where he cites Isaiah 59:20–21 and 27:9, and to Christ's ministry of salvation to the Gentiles in Romans 15:12, where he cites Isaiah 11:1 and 10. We can note further:

* Romans 11:34 cites Isaiah 40:13 in exalting the wisdom of God.

* Romans 14:11 cites Isaiah 45:23 in insisting that everyone, weak and strong, is subject to the judgment of God.

* Romans 2:24 cites Isaiah 52:5, Romans 3:15-17 cites Isaiah 59:7-8, and Romans 10:20-21 cites Isaiah 65:1-2 in affirming the wickedness of unbelievers.

* Romans 10:15-16 cites Isaiah 52:7 and 53:1 to describe the apostles who share the gospel.

And as with the citations in the Gospels, some of these passages are central to Paul's argument, while others offer simply an enrichment of his rhetoric. All this is as one might expect.[6]

THE EARLY CHRISTIAN CENTURIES

If we could survey the long Christian tradition in the period after the New Testament, we would continue to see Isaiah used in all the ways we have already glimpsed. The tradition becomes richer, but there are no fresh departures until modern times. Accordingly I shall simply offer the merest hint of this tradition.

The Church Fathers continued to work with the Christian approaches to Isaiah as laid out by the New Testament. The *Epistle of Barnabas*, written at the end of the first century or early in the second, is a teaching work for the newly baptized that is only a bit shorter than the Letter to the Romans. The author maintains that the Old Testament was intended for Christians from the very beginning. In the course of the work he offers twenty-four citations from Isaiah. These citations mostly follow the Septuagint when it differs from the Hebrew text. The citations are often not word-for-word but may instead have been taken from a collection of testimonials. For example, chapter 9 begins, "For again, he [God] speaks concerning the ears, how he circumcised the ears of our heart." After this, in the short space of ten lines, he cites a verse from the Psalms, then Isaiah 33:13 in the Septuagint text, "By hearing, those who are far off shall hearken; the things I have done will become known." After this he paraphrases Jeremiah 4:4, "And circumcise, says the Lord, your hearts," and, after a couple of passages adapting various Old Testament texts, he paraphrases three passages from Isaiah, "Hear, heaven, and give ear, earth; for the

Lord has spoken" (1:2), "Hear the Lord's word, rulers of this people" (1:10), and "Hear, children, a voice crying in the desert" (40:3).[7]

Jerome (ca. 342–420 CE), one of the great scholars in Christian history, made a fresh translation of the Old Testament into Latin, the translation that became standard for Roman Catholics (the Vulgate). Beyond his translation work, he wrote commentaries on many books of the Bible, struggling critically with difficult texts. Among his commentaries is one on Isaiah. He expends almost twelve hundred words on Isaiah 6:9–10, that passage in which Isaiah understands God calling to him to obfuscate the message. As we have seen, these verses have given trouble to many commentators.[8] Here Jerome is fully aware of the theological difficulty caused by God seeming to be responsible for the people's blindness.

Jerome's comment on the passage falls into two parts. First, since the contrast between the Hebrew text and the Septuagint is particularly glaring in this passage (the Septuagint, as we noted in Chapter 7, simply predicts the people's blindness, not affirming the responsibility of God), he deals not only with the problem of the contrast between the two text traditions in this specific passage, but more generally with the way in which, in the various books of the New Testament, the authors sometimes cite the form of text found in the Hebrew text tradition, and sometimes cites the Septuagintal readings, where they differ. He begins by discussing Acts 28:25–28, which cites the passage in question. Here Luke, the author of Acts, describes Paul in debate with the Jews. In this debate Paul cites the Isaiah verses in the Septuagint form. Jerome points out that one might argue that Luke prefers the Septuagint because, after all, his specialization is medicine, and he offers a splendid Greek style. Thus one cannot argue for

Luke's choice of the Septuagint in the Acts passage based solely on Luke's personal preference. However, when citing the Old Testament, both Matthew and John use, sometimes one tradition, sometimes the other. He then offers several examples of this phenomenon, among them Matthew 2:15, which cites Hosea 11:1 in the Hebrew rather than the Septuagint, and John 19:37, which cites Zechariah 12:10, again in the Hebrew rather than the Septuagint. As to the argument used by some in Jerome's day that the Jews later falsified their Scriptures to bring about these awkward disparities, he says the argument merits a horselaugh (*cacchinum*). As if the Savior, and the evangelists and apostles, would cite Old Testament passages when the Jews were going to falsify them. Thus he rejects the easy solution to the problem presented by Isaiah 6:9–10, of simply following the Septuagint text here.

The second part of his comment on the passage deals with the Hebrew text itself. He begins by citing other equally harsh passages. In Exodus 9:16 God, through Moses, addresses Pharaoh with the words, "This is why I have let you live, to show you my power," a statement directly following God's word on hardening Pharaoh's heart (v. 12; Jerome points out that in this passage the Septuagint is just as harsh as the Hebrew text is). This treatment is not confined to Pharaoh. Jerome cites Romans 11:8, where Paul writes, "As it is written, 'God gave them a sluggish spirit, eyes that would not see and ears that would not hear, down to this very day.'" (There is no Old Testament text quite like this. The presumed citation has in it elements of Deuteronomy 29:4 and Isaiah 29:10.) Jerome also cites a passage in the psalms, "Let their table be a trap for them, a snare for their allies. Let their eyes be darkened so that they cannot see, and make their loins tremble continually" (in Protestant translations the passage is Psalm 69:22-23). In these texts it is God who is responsible, not the people themselves, for their having eyes and not seeing. Churches must therefore come to terms with all such passages, not with the Isaiah passage alone.

Jerome then returns to Romans 11 for his explanation. In verse after verse of that chapter, Paul explains how God has hardened some that he may be merciful to all (v. 32), and Jerome concludes, "Therefore it is not the cruelty of God but mercy that one nation perish so that all may be saved." He closes his comments by citing the words of Jesus, after the healing of the man born blind (John 9:39), "I came into this world for judgment so that those who do not see may see, and those who do see may become blind," and with the words of Jesus over Jerusalem in Matthew 23:37, "How often have I desired to gather your children together as a hen gathers her brood under her wings, and you were not willing."

Jerome's comments may not be altogether adequate to present-day readers who are attentive to biblical faith, but Paul's discourse in his Letter to the Romans does remind them that the more general puzzle remains. How one may square divine sovereignty wth human will both for good and for evil. Jerome at least sees what the issue is.

THE SIXTEENTH TO EIGHTEENTH CENTURIES

Martin Luther (1483–1546) inaugurated the Protestant Reformation. Beyond his work as a reformer Luther is remembered largely for his translation of the Bible into German. But fully as important were his lectures on books of the Bible. He lectured on Isaiah from 1527 to 1530 and then returned to that prophet and lectured on chapters 9 and 53 during the last few years of his life.[9]

Luther's commentaries are deeply informed by the warmth of his own experience. He "owed to the Vulgate translation of Isaiah the formulas by which the mystery of divine action and nature seemed to him from the very beginning to be expressed in an incomparable manner: the word about the strange work through which God performs his own work (Isaiah 28:21) and the 'hidden God' (*Deus absconditus*) (Isaiah 45:15)." On Isaiah 54:7, "God said, For a brief moment I forsook you." Luther takes hope from the fact that God's action of forsaking is only for a brief moment: "This is a very beautiful consolation, of which I have made frequent use."[10]

In dealing with Isaiah 6:9–10 Luther avoids all questions of predestination and the consequent question of God's deliberate hardening of the people. With regard to v. 9, "Go and say to this people," he points out:

> The emphasis lies on His saying "this," not "My," as if He were saying "rejected," "accursed." We do not here wish anxiously to torture ourselves regarding the secret will of God, but only to set forth those matters concerning the mood of God and of His preachers. For God is justly angry with the stubborn who please themselves and have no desire to learn to know themselves and to deny themselves. It is to them that this must be said with displeasure: *Hear and hear, but do not understand, etc.*, and they must at last be abandoned.

He then refers to the passages of the Gospels that cite the passage in various phrasings, applying it, as one might anticipate, to the Jews. He concludes his remarks with his well-known contrast between faith and works:

> The ungodly are irked by much preaching, especially by the preaching of faith in opposition to works, but this preaching must nevertheless not be omitted because of them. Here the prophet in no way argues

about the will of predestination, but only about God's attitude against the hardened, that they must be forsaken.

Luther does not, of course, assume more than one author for the book of Isaiah, but at the beginning of his lecture on chapter 40 he notes matter-of-factly that Isaiah is divided into two books at this point.

> In the following book the prophet treats two matters: Prophecies concerning Christ the King and then concerning Cyrus, King of Persia, and concerning the Babylonian captivity. This second book is nothing but prophecy, first external, concerning King Cyrus, and then spiritual, concerning Christ. And here the prophet is the most joyful of all, fairly dancing with promises. The next four chapters prophesy the most joyful things concerning Christ and the church in our time.

In regard to the phrase "Comfort, comfort my people" (40:1), he remarks that "*My* has the accent, as if to say, 'I have a people which I will not forsake.'" This is in nice contrast to his remark cited above on "*this* people" in 6:9.

John Calvin (1509–64) is the second giant of the Reformation, remembered both for his theological work (*The Institutes of the Christian Religion*) and for his biblical commentaries. His commentary on Isaiah, dedicated to Edward VI of England, was originally published in 1550; in the standard English translation it covers almost eighteen hundred pages.[11]

We have already encountered a portion of Calvin's treatment of Isaiah 61:1 (see Chapter 1), in which he points out that the words refer both to the prophet himself and to Jesus Christ. It is most noteworthy that God's call to Isaiah, in 6:9–10, to render the people insensitive does not dismay. He understands God to have warned Isaiah, saying in effect, "You will indeed teach without any good effect, but do not regret your teaching, for I enjoin it upon you. Do not refrain from teaching, because it yields no advantage. Only obey me, and leave to my disposal all the consequences of your labours." Calvin speaks of his own experience in preaching, "We too have experienced it more than we could have wished; but it has been shared by all the servants of Christ, and therefore we ought to endure it with greater patience, though it is a very grievous stumbling-block to those who serve God with a pure conscience." Then Calvin invokes predestination, but gently.

> Yet if you inquire into the first cause, we must come to the predestination of God. But as that purpose is hidden from us, we must not too eagerly search into it; for the everlasting scheme of the divine purpose is beyond our reach, but we ought to consider the cause which lies plainly before our eyes, namely, the rebellion by which they rendered themselves unworthy of blessings so numerous and great.

Several times in the course of this study I have mentioned *Messiah* of George Frederick Handel (1685-1759). Ever since its first performance in 1742 it has been a primary channel through which the Isaiah texts of Christian importance have come through to the English-speaking world. *Messiah* has three parts. In the Part One (the "Christmas" section), one hears Isaiah 40:1–5, followed by passages from Haggai and Malachi, followed by Isaiah 7:14; 40:9; 9:2–3, 6, followed by passages of Luke and a passage of Zechariah, and closing with Isaiah 35:5–6; 40:11, and a passage of Matthew. In Part Two (with texts associated with Lent and Easter) one hears Isaiah 53:3; 50:6; 53:4–6, 8, interspersed with passages of the Psalms, Lamentations and books of the New Testament. The short

Part Three, aside from two verses of Job, contains only passages from the New Testament. In Handel's oratorio key passages from Isaiah have come into a perfect musical synthesis with New Testament affirmations.

CURRENT WORK ON ISAIAH

Modern scholarly work on the book of Isaiah began a little more than two centuries ago. There is no way in a work of this compass to survey it.[12] Suffice it to say that there is no book of the Old Testament over which Christians have struggled more than Isaiah. The struggle has focused on two main issues: first, whether one is to translate the contested noun in Isaiah 7:14 as "virgin," to conform to Matthew 1:23, or as "young woman," and second, whether one is to recognize more than one author for the book. The struggle over these issues has vexed Catholics and Protestants equally. I shall give two specifics on the struggle, the Catholics on multiple authorship and the Protestants on Isaiah 7:14.

Roman Catholics, in the Pontifical Biblical Commission in 1908, in respond to the question (couched in ponderous style): "Whether the philological argument, one derived from the language and the style, and employed to impugn the identity of the author of the book of Isaias [Isaiah], is to be considered weighty eough to compel a man of judgment versed in the principles of criticism and well acquainted with Hebrew, to acknowledge in the same book a plurality of authors." The answer: "In the negative."[13]

On Isaiah 7:14, the Protestant Revised Standard Version translated the noun in question as "a young woman," with a footnote "Or *virgin*," but even with the footnote, the appearance of this translation in 1952 set off an immense furor. Luther Weigle, chair of the committee that produced the translation, preserved in a coffee can the ashes of an RSV Bible sent to him by a radio evangelist who was pastor of the Furnace Street Mission in Akron, Ohio. The can in question was passed down to Herbert Gordon May, who was chair of the committee that produced the New Revised Standard Version (I myself have seen it!). Indeed the translation of Isaiah 7:14 was one of the main stimuli for the publication of the New International Version.[14] And even the New Revised Standard Version, published in 1989, though it changed "a young woman" to "the young woman" (which is closer to the Hebrew text), retained a footnote. It now reads "Gk *the virgin.*"

Fortunately biblical scholarship has moved ahead in recent decades in spite of these church struggles. Thanks to various developments within Roman Catholicism, especially the Second Vatican Council, it is now normal within that communion to believe in more than one Isaiah. And Protestants in the RSV tradition have become accustomed to "a (or the) young woman" (as have Catholics, too, one may add).[15]

As a symbol of Christian scholarship for the turn of the millennium one may cite the new commentary on Isaiah by Brevard S. Childs.[16] Childs has been one of the outstanding Old Testament scholars in the second half of the twentieth century. After receiving degrees from the University of Michigan, Princeton Theological Seminary, and the University of Basel (Switzerland), he began teaching at Yale University in 1958 and retired in 1999. One of his early publications dealt with the original Isaiah: *Isaiah and the Assyrian Crisis* (1967).[17] He is one of the few in our day who have explored the theological meaning of both the Old and New Testament, separately and together, having published *Introduction to the Old Testament as Scripture* (1979), *The*

New Testament as Canon: An Introduction (1984), and *Biblical Theology of the Old and New Testaments* (1993).[18] His "canonical criticism" has not met with universal appreciation. Many critics accuse him of scanting the significance of the historical particularity of individual biblical texts,[19] but he at least attempts to view the biblical witness as a totality.

His commentary on Isaiah, a work of 555 pages, views the prophetic book as a whole, stressing how the sixty-six chapters function in their finished form. He is particularly sensitive to the way later layers of the tradition both cite and modify earlier layers. As for Isaiah in the New Testament, he is thoroughly aware of how it has taken up the witness of the book of Isaiah.

> Regarding the place of the New Testament in an Old Testament commentary on Isaiah, the primary task of the latter is to hear the Old Testament's own discrete voice and to honor its own theological integrity. Yet as a Christian interpreter, I confess with the church that the Old and New Testaments, in their distinct canonical forms, together form a theological whole. However, to deal adequately with the New Testament far exceeds the scope an an Old Testament commentary and the ability of this author.[20]

To me this program offers the ideal blend of sensitivity and modesty.

AN AFTERWORD ON ISLAM

Now, at the end of our quest, I turn for the merest glance at the third of the monotheistic faiths derived from Abraham, namely Islam. Although the Qur'an does mention several biblical figures,[21] Isaiah is not among them. Nevertheless Isaiah (Arabic *Sha'ya*) is well known in the

Muslim literature called "legends of the prophets," particularly because he is understood to have predicted the coming of both Jesus and Muhammad. According to one account, Isaiah was a prophet sent to the Israelites in the reign of Zedekiah (here there is a confusion with Hezekiah). He took part in the siege of Jerusalem under Sennacherib, and he announced to the king that, because God had heard his prayer, his death had been postponed for fifteen years. God then destroyed all the enemy forces except Sennacherib and five scribes. After parading them around Jerusalem for sixty-six days, Zedekiah followed the command of God and allowed Sennacherib to return to Babylon.[22]

From the point of view of history it is clear that Muhammad had contacts with Christians and Jews both during the travels he undertook as a young man before his prophetic call, and in his later career as well.[23] Jewish and Christian lore thus entered into Muslim tradition through Muhammad himself and through later Muslim traditionists. We are confronted with a remarkable situation. In Chapter 2 we affirmed that we know almost nothing about the historical Isaiah. Yet the name (and fame) of this prophet, and various affirmations made about him, have circulated among Jews and Christians in both oral and written form for centuries, finally lodging even in the tradition of Islam, whose faith denies altogether the accuracy and finality of the Bible. This circumstance in itself is testimony to the reach of one of the great figures of monotheistic faith. Unbound by time, place, *and* tradition, Isaiah does indeed still speak.

NOTES

1. If multiple citations of a single passage in the Synoptic Gospels are reckoned as a single citation (e.g. Isaiah 14:13, 15 in Matthew

11:23 and Luke 10:15), one authority counts 184 citations from Isaiah. Citations from the Psalms total 186, but the text of the Psalms is roughly twenty per cent longer than Isaiah. See Erwin Nestle, ed., *Novum Testamentum Graece*, 21st ed. (Stuttgart: Privilegierte Württembergische Bibelanstalt, 1952), 662–67.

2. Craig A. Evans, "From Gospel to Gospel, The Function of Isaiah in the New Testament," in *Writing and Reading the Scroll of Isaiah Studies of an Interpretive Tradition* (ed. Craig C. Broyles and Craig A. Evans; Supplements to the Vetus Testamentum 70; Leiden: Brill, 1997), 653–67.

3. Evans, "From Gospel to Gospel," 674.

4. See Reginald H. Fuller, *The Mission and Achievement of Jesus* (Studies in Biblical Theology 12; Chicago: Alec R. Allenson, 1956), 50–78, esp. 77–78; and, in less detail, John P. Meier, "Jesus," in Raymond E. Brown, Joseph A. Fitzmyer and Roland E. Murphy (eds.), *The New Jerome Biblical Commentary* (Englewood Cliffs, NJ: Prentice Hall, 1990), 1323, 1326; compare Raymond E. Brown, *The Death of the Messiah* (New York: Doubleday, 1994), 1485–87. Compare also the recent collection of essays in William H. Bellinger, Jr., and William R. Farmer (eds.), *Jesus and the Suffering Servant: Isaiah 53 and Christian Origins* (Harrisburg, PA: Trinity, 1998).

5. John P. Meier, *A Marginal Jew, Rethinking the Historical Jesus* 2 (New York: Doubleday, 1994), 491–92; compare Vincent Taylor, *The Gospel According to St. Mark* (London: Macmillan, 1959), 255–58.

6. For a survey of Paul's use of Isaiah see Evans, "From Gospel to Gospel," 682–91.

7. I have used the Greek text in J. B. Lightfoot, *The Apostoic Fathers* (London/New York: Macmillan, 1898), 239–88, and quoted the English translation in Robert A. Kraft, *The Apostolic Fathers, a New Translation and Commentary*: Vol. 3, *Barnabas and the Didache* (New York: Nelson, 1965), 106–7; for the background see Kraft, 17–56.

8. I have used the Latin text in J. Migne, *Patrologia Latina*, Vol. 24, columns 100-2.

9. See Heinrich Bornkamm, *Luther and the Old Testament* (German original 1948; English transl., Philadelphia: Fortress Press, 1969) 31. For Luther's lectures of 1527-30 see the English transl. in *Luther's Works*, Vols. 16, 17 (St. Louis: Concordia, 1972). The later lectures on Isaiah 9, first published in 1543-44, and on Isaiah 53, first published in 1544, 1546, and 1550, can be found in German in *D. Mar-*

tin Luthers Werke (Weimar: 1883-), 40:III 595-682 and 683-746 respectively.

10. For these two comments see Bornkamm, *Luther and the Old Testament*, 9.

11. John Calvin, *Commentary on the Book of the Prophet Isaiah* (Edinburgh: Constable, 1850–54), often reprinted.

12. A useful review may be found in Brevard S. Childs, *Introduction to the Old Testament as Scripture* (Philadelphia: Fortress Press, 1979), 316–25.

13. The original text is in Latin. For the English translation see *Rome and the Study of Scripture* (St. Meinrad, IN: Grail, 1962), 119.

14. An eminently readable account of the whole matter may be found in Peter J. Thuesen, *In Discordance with the Scriptures: American Protestant Battles over Translating the Bible* (New York/Oxford: Oxford University Press, 1999), esp. chap. 4; for the matter of the ashes, see there p. 97.

15. For current Catholic scholarship on the question see Joseph Jensen and William H. Irwin, C. S. B., "Isaiah 1–39," *The New Jerome Biblical Commentary*, 235.

16. Brevard S. Childs, *Isaiah* (Old Testament Library; Louisville, KY: Westminster John Knox, 2001).

17. Brevard S. Childs, *Isaiah and the Assyrian Crisis* (Studies in Biblical Theology, Second Series 3; Naperville, IL: Alec R. Allenson, 1967).

18. Brevard S. Childs, *Introduction to the Old Testament as Scripture* (Philadelphia: Fortress, 1979); *The New Testament as Canon: An Introduction* (Philadelphia: Fortress, 1984); *Biblical Theology of the Old and New Testament: Theological Reflection on the Christian Bible* (Minneapolis: Fortress, 1993).

19. For a careful current assessment of Childs's approach, see Walter Brueggemann, *Theology of the Old Testament: Testimony, Dispute, Advocacy* (Minneapolis: Fortress Press, 1997), 89–93. Walter Harrelson expressed his "exasperation" at Childs's approach in his review of *Introduction to the Old Testament as Scripture* in *Journal of Biblical Literature* 100 (1981), 99–103.

20. Childs, *Isaiah*, 4–5.

21. Qur'an 3:33 mentions Adam, Noah, and Abraham; Mary and Zechariah are mentioned in 3:36-3-7; John the Baptist in 3:39; and

Jesus in 3:45. 3:84 mentions Abraham, Ishmael, Isaac, Jacob, Moses, Jesus and "the Prophets." There are many other such references.

22. See the entries "Sha'yā" *The Encyclopaedia of Islam* 4 (Leiden: Brill, 1913–38), 343; and *The Encyclopaedia of Islam,* New Edition 9 (Leiden: Brill, 1960), 382–83.

23. Tor Andrae, *Mohammed, The Man and His Faith* (New York: Barnes and Noble, 1935), 13–52.

Index to Biblical Passages